NEVER ENOUGH ZEROES

A Memoir

D0792591

JOEL SOPER

with Philip Wyeth

This book is memoir. It reflects the author's present recollections of experiences over time. Some names and characteristics have been changed, some events have been compressed, and some dialogue has been recreated.

www.neverenoughzeroes.com

Front cover design by Philip Wyeth and Josh Madson.

Book layout and design by Philip Wyeth.
www.philipwyeth.com

CONTENTS

INTRODUCTION

I don't claim to be a good man, or someone you should admire. While my life has certainly been exciting, it very well could have ended badly half a dozen times in the past. And if my compulsive gambling is what got me into all that trouble, then I have to credit my verbal skills for helping me talk my way out of each dangerous situation.

You've heard the saying that the house always wins. Some people also say that God always wins. I believe both are true because I'm living proof. The more good I did in life, the more God would reward me. But the more I gambled, the more money I lost while also bringing more trouble into my life.

Hi, I'm Joel. The best salesman and worst sports better you'll ever meet. I've made millions with my silver tongue and then lost it all in heartbreaking fashion countless times. I've been threatened, beaten, and homeless, yet somehow lived to tell the tale.

I'm sharing my story with you and the world for several reasons. First, I think it's an interesting real-life tale that a lot of people will get a kick out of. It's also my attempt to own up to my faults and write a new chapter for the second half of my life. I hope that my struggle and my journey will help others who are consumed by this scourge which is a silent killer compared to the addictions that leave more visible traces.

Being a gambler means you have to accept the trifecta of losing time, money, and people. That's right, chasing all those big dreams ends up making your world smaller than you ever thought possible.

Sometimes you're forced out of your modest house into a dingy apartment that's even further away from the mansion you've been fantasizing about. Years of your life disappear in the blink of an eye despite those many days and nights filled with thrilling action and desperate worry.

Then you find yourself sitting alone in the dark tapping away at the little black rectangle which has become the focal point of your existence. Inside that inscrutable electronic device resides all of your hopes and nightmares, as the distant sporting events displayed on the screen as betting odds and ticking game clocks hold your fate in the balance. Win and you're dancing – lose and you curse the gods.

Either way, it's a lock that you'll be back tomorrow to cast your next paycheck into that shimmering wishing well of temptation, because you can't ever leave well enough alone...

In some ways our story is as old as time itself. It serves as a warning in the great religious books and is passed down from generation to generation through fairy tales and fables. But I guess part of the reason for living is to burn your fingertips on the stove now and again – to test the limits of what the world *says* you can and can't do.

I've tried to be the Icarus of sports betting for two-thirds of my life, and no matter how many times I crash into the sea, I always brush off my wings and fly toward the sun once again. Because I'm greedy and reckless and proud, plus all the other sins that we're warned against by proverbs and medieval literature.

In other words, I'm all too human.

I'm not content with my lot in life or the status quo. I yearn to be celebrated and live in the lap of luxury as an end in itself, rather than as a reward for seeing plans through to the end in the name of accomplishing great deeds. I am forever the hare finding ways to lose to the tortoise – because I want the glory more than I'm willing to do the work.

I can now confirm after more than a quarter century of trying, that if there ever was a shortcut to success and happiness, it no longer exists. It's the one thing I've committed to achieving with constant and diligent effort, only to come up empty in a million different ways.

So now I'm taking a different approach. Creating something from the heart to give to others with no expectations, while also hoping that I might finally get off this treadmill and sleep soundly at night. To know that I'm not alone anymore because my story mirrors your own – and perhaps together we can find peace and forge a new path for our lives.

There's no shame in walking away from gambling without having captured that ultimate prize which exists in our mind's eye. The professional athletes we bet on often have little say in the matter when their own time comes – the combination of age, injuries, and the endless crop of new talent forces them to one day hang up the cleats and retire. If they have the grace to carry on with their lives away from the cheering crowds, then surely we can find the strength to stop the cycle of painful self-sabotage that the rest of the world is oblivious to.

Even if we're not quite capable of *building* anything, for now it's probably enough to set down the pistol we've been madly firing at our own feet. To be still instead of constantly scheming, thankful rather than covetous, and living in the moment without getting lost in another impossible daydream.

But that doesn't mean you have to withdraw to the solitude of some remote monastery up in the mountains. Why? Because I still want to be rich and famous! That's right, at the end of the day I really *do* want to be known for something. Just because you've been chastened doesn't mean you have to call the doctor to schedule a frontal lobotomy.

There's still a lot of *life* pumping through my veins. I've got a compulsive personality and I can't just turn it off. What I *haven't* been able to do all this time is try something new – until now!

So hop in and take a ride on the roller coaster I've been living ever since I placed that first "sure thing" bet on a pony back in Detroit, Michigan, all those years ago…

1. JOHNNY APPLESEED

Any neighborhood you visit in San Diego or Los Angeles, chances are you'll see a yard that's green and lush because of me. Because of my system and my team. But most of all, because I've got the verbal skills that pay the bills.

I like to build rapport with prospective customers, getting to know them as real people before going in for the kill. Because it's not really that. You're making a genuine connection with them in order to make the sale. It's an important distinction that people notice on a subconscious level, and is often the factor that distinguishes the successful businessman from the salesman who's just getting by.

After the close is when I set the gears of my operation into motion. I've got teams of reliable guys all over the area that show up on time and get the job done right. I pay them handsomely to ensure that it all runs like a well-oiled machine.

Southern California is home to a lot of wealthy people.

I have clients that are worth tens of millions of dollars, and they won't even flinch when I ask them to write me a check for fifty grand to install a new sprinkler system on their property.

Most of them probably think I'm rolling in dough with a nice house of my own in Encino or Studio City. I would be, and I really should be, but pretty much every dollar that's left over after the cost of doing business goes to feed my gambling habit.

And that's the paradox: part of the reason I work so damn hard is to get the money I need for the day's bets or to pay back the bookies that I owe. So if it weren't for my hustle, how many thousands of homes would have ugly yards and wasteful watering systems?

For thirty years I've been a veritable Johnny Appleseed carving out a mini-green revolution across the drought-plagued Southland region. All because I'm so hooked on sports betting that as soon as any money enters my grasp, I literally black out and drive in a semi-hypnotic state to my bookie's place. I then eagerly hand him the cash, which is usually never to be seen again.

I might be the most societally productive gambler of the twenty-first century. Who else has beautified the world more than I have in the name of fueling their sick sports obsession? I don't rob banks or sell heroin! No, instead I increase the value of people's homes while reducing citywide annual water usage by millions of gallons a year... while *I* lose millions of dollars.

Water wise... and pound foolish! Yeah, that's me. Always doing things vicariously and living life one step removed. Working on someone else's yard. Betting on games being played by others – not by me or my own kids.

But why? Do I just want to be unattached and free? Is it a secret self-loathing or fatalistic undertow that wants to drag me out to sea? Maybe I live a form of schizophrenia where my day is compartmentalized into Seller Joel, Cash-in-Hand Zombie Joel, Thrill-seeking Gambler Joel, and finally Baffled and Broke Joel.

I can tell you this, though. I've been living that *Groundhog Day* life for too damn long and now I'm tired. It's really breaking me down.

Which is maybe why I started writing this book. Throwing myself a lifeline to break out of the loop that's turned into a blur. It's a recurring nightmare where I always know what's going to happen: be successful at my job, then get the equal and opposite negative result with my bets.

Money in, money out. Drive here to collect, drive there to drop it off. Doing the same thing over and over. Stuck on the treadmill as my energy level slowly drains away to nothing…

But now I have this book and you're reading it. I finally went at life directly and ended up creating something that's not only my own but also completely new! It's the first manifestation of a desire which I've probably had for a long time, but could just never see clearly or focus on to pursue.

What did it take to start forging a fresh path? Not all the times I got myself into dangerous situations, that's for sure. Even when I thought I was going to die, there was still something savory about that feeling of visceral terror, the adrenaline rush of living out a scene from a movie in real life.

Nope, I just had to believe that there could be another way to live, that I could change course and take a different road from here on out.

So now I'll let someone else tend to the lawn care needs of Southern California while I enjoy my own yard. I'll spend my money on sports equipment for the Little League team I'm coaching, rather than flush it down the drain on games happening in other time zones.

If I could do it, then so can you. You're not alone, even if we all have our own struggles and unique life path.

Change is possible for each and every one of us. We have to remember that it's a jagged mountain rife with inevitable setbacks, but all we have to do is keep moving forward.

Growth comes from struggle, and courage is the fuel. So let it burn and let your journey be the light that inspires the next person to change their own life for the better.

See you at the top.

8

2. NEVER ENOUGH ZEROES

Here's the thing about being a compulsive gambler –
there's never enough zeroes.

I've had weeks where I won a hundred thousand
dollars. Did I treat myself to a vacation in Palm Springs?
Nope. Did I buy a new car? No, sir.

What happens when I'm flush with cash is that I
increase the amount of each wager. For example, if I
normally bet five hundred on a particular game, now it'll
be a thousand. So I can win *more*, get that rush and feel
the *thrill* of winning again.

That's really what it is. All that it is. Which is why I
say forget the money. If some aunt dies and leaves me
half a million tax-free, unless that value's locked up in a
trust or an actual piece of real estate, then I'll just use it as
principal on my next bet. And the next hundred bets after
that.

What's so frustrating is how at the end of the day, I'm
always the one left with nothing. I wake up early and
drive out to some rich producer's house in the Hollywood

Hills. I close the deal and they cut me a check for ten, twenty, thirty thousand without batting an eye. The work we're going to do will beautify their property, reduce their water bill, and in the end increase the value of their home.

Next, my crew. I only hire the most dedicated guys and pay them well. They get the job done day in and day out for me, so I make sure they earn enough money to feed their families. Now they all live in big houses and drive new trucks while I don't even have a car.

The girl who works in the office handling leads and the paperwork, she's getting paid plenty too. All my materials suppliers get their cut as well.

And that big pile of money that's left over for me? It just slips through my fingers...

Every game being played is like a little baggie of heroin. My week ends up looking like a block on Skid Row. Everywhere you turn someone's sprawled out on the ground, and each one of them is me after losing a bet.

Fifteen hundred on the Lakers-Mavs game. Three hundred on the second period of the Blackhawks versus the Bruins. And another hundred on Chinese women's basketball simply because I couldn't sleep at midnight.

So who's got my money? Scumbags. Sometimes they run a little mom-and-pop restaurant as a tax front. Some of them offer a little side action out of a legit poker room. Others I never even meet because they host a gambling website that's based overseas.

But they all have one thing in common. They've got no problem laying out that piece of cheese for me – and every time, like some animal that's too dumb to ever learn, I go for the bait.

And no matter how battered, bruised, or miserable I

am, as long as I have a few crumpled dollar bills in my hand, they never turn me away. No pity, no compassion, no shred of *humanity* to say no for my own good.

Why? Because they're just as greedy as I am. Sitting on the opposite side of a table that's made of rotten wood.

It's hell, honestly. We're in hell, the lot of us. Chasing after vicarious thrills taking place in arenas we'll never set foot upon ourselves. Moments of athletic glory we pollute by carving them up with rusty scalpels.

Plus-7 to cover the spread. Two or more hits for the cleanup hitter. A 55-yard field goal before halftime that's glorious not because the kicker was on the practice squad a few weeks ago, but because those three points put an extra two grand in our pocket.

It's disgusting. We're disgusting. But saying it isn't enough, you know? We're trapped in a maze living the same day for years on end.

Athletes come and go. Playing for one team this season, then signing on as a free agent or retiring the next. I don't even care because they're just like cards in a deck on a night of twenty poker hands.

These sports heroes have the power to make or break my week – but not my heart. Because I'm not a kid anymore, right? All the Detroit teams I loved growing up – the Pistons, the Red Wings, the Lions and Tigers – they don't matter as much to me now. So if the Pistons lose and I win money, or if they win but not by *enough*, so that I lose money…

I've cut my soul out of sports and replaced it with my own personal chase. I pursue it while sitting alone in some Starbucks in the San Fernando Valley. Or I've got the game stats updating on my cell phone while driving out to a client on the 101 Freeway. I'll see a goal scored out of the corner of my eye and get a little thrill. Cash for me, yeah.

I used to be a hell of a soccer player myself back in the day. The feeling I got after sending one past the goalie from thirty yards out, now that was pure. You can't bottle it, that's for sure. So you close your eyes and chase after it for the rest of your life, hoping to catch another whiff of running across a dewy green field in April, to relive that bittersweet memory from a simpler time that's so far removed from reality...

Because all those professionals you see on TV? It isn't so pure for them anymore, either. They've got big contracts, plus endorsement deals with merch brands and car insurance companies. They've got secret girlfriends with expensive tastes or ex-wives who take a cut of their salary each month. They've got back spasms and an unlicensed pain-pill dealer so they can hopefully eke out an extra season or two in the starting lineup.

What I'm saying is that when it comes to sports, it's all in our heads. We make of it whatever we want it to mean – and none of us can turn our eyes away. As that spiraling football arcs majestically toward the open wide receiver, we collectively hold our breath for a million different reasons.

The father of the quarterback wondering if his kid has what it takes for a real career. The assistant whose wife has been pressuring him to land a head-coaching job somewhere else. The old man in the stands still holding out hope that he'll see a championship banner raised before he dies.

There's also the concession stand worker who needs the team to make the playoffs so she can make rent. The local sports columnist who once aspired to write great novels and now pours his heart into each piece, clinging to the belief that *one* reader might have the power to pluck him out of obscurity.

Then come the restaurant owners who pay for the sports package so people will spend their Saturdays at the bar. The guys sitting on those stools, each nursing a beer and their thoughts, their own dramas and dreams...

Every one of them is caught up in this breathless moment that's suspended in time...

Will he make the catch or not?

I want to be able to feel it the way it was meant to again. I'm spilling my guts and speaking so frankly because I know you can't beat addiction alone.

You need a team.

3. WHO'S TO BLAME?

A lot of people who lead messed up lives can lay the blame on a rough upbringing. Tales of violence, abuse, all kinds of horrific trauma… they never had a chance.

But not me! My childhood growing up in the suburbs during the 1970s was fantastic. Around forty kids my age lived in the subdivision and there was always something going on in the neighborhood, be it a game of street hockey or a backyard barbecue.

My parents are great people without a blemish to their name. Same goes for my two brothers and one sister, all very successful and living clean lives. My sister has bailed me out so many times over the years that if not for her, guaranteed I'd be in jail or dead by now.

I'm the baby of the family by several years, so if anything maybe they coddled me a bit too much. But most guys coming from sheltered backgrounds either just coast through life or shape up after an encounter with gritty reality gives them a rude awakening. Again, not for yours truly!

I gravitated to the wild side early on, so by the time the first warning signs of real danger appeared, I was already too hooked to care, listen, or learn.

At age sixteen I was running around Detroit as an errand boy for one of the local bookies, a guy named Lou who taught me all the ropes. I was in the action and making cash money while my classmates were flipping burgers or changing engine oil for minimum wage. Thanks, but no thanks!

Everybody bet on sports back in those days, although the only person in my family that gambled was my grandfather Joseph. He passed away when I was less than a year old so I can't say he's the one who got me hooked, but they do say these things skip a generation. There's actually a photo of him holding me as a baby, and I have to admit he's definitely one person I wish I could have gotten to know.

Like me, my grandfather also got in over his head with gambling debts, and he ended up embezzling money from the sporting goods store he owned. The loan sharks would drop in for chats and set him up on payment plans using the business as collateral.

One day he died while walking home from the racetrack. They said it was a heart attack, and I never thought to question the story until recently. In a way it's kind of romantic, a man dying after spending an afternoon at the place he loved betting on the ponies.

It's not very pleasant to consider the alternatives, but now that I'm older and a seasoned gambler myself, I can't help but wonder if maybe his debts got so out of hand that someone whacked him. What if the bookie had his guys tail my grandfather until the perfect opportunity arose to kill him?

Would accepting that possibility make me stop gambling? Let's be real here. I've been punched, cornered, even had one of my dogs taken hostage and still didn't quit.

The only luck I've had in all these years of gambling is avoiding the comeuppance I've been provoking and probably deserve. So many times I could have died but somehow I always managed to talk my way out of it. I could have gone to prison on several occasions as well, but there was always a personal connection or legal loophole that worked in my favor to lessen the blow. In that regard I truly consider myself the luckiest person on earth.

I do wish I could take it all back, though. I wish I'd never met Lou, even if he seemed like a mentor to me at the time when I was an impressionable kid. I watched everything he did, from taking the bets to collecting the money. He was cold-blooded and taught me how to be cold-blooded.

The one thing I'm really mad about is that he told me to bet the underdogs and the under, because the suckers in the general public always bet the favorites and the over. That may have been true way back when, but now sports have become very fan-oriented and people want to see a lot of scoring.

Back in the '80s, a baseball final score of 2-1 was common. NBA games would end 88-84 all the time. But now, the Dodgers will beat the Padres 11-9, and NFL results look more like college football when the scoreboard says 42-35.

Clearly the trend is for games to go over, but I just can't break free from Lou's advice because I keep thinking I'm due. All these years later and I'm still haunted by his words, it's a nightmare!

So even if it's true that my grandfather Joseph really did die of a heart attack, there's no doubt I'm running toward a similar fate because I am definitely not living the right way. This is what gambling does to a person: you grind yourself down through mental stress and neglect your health because all you can think about is the next bet. You eat like garbage, don't go to the gym, barely get enough sleep, and rile yourself up into an emotional frenzy a dozen times an hour from dawn to dusk.

Plus there's no days off. It's not like you personally are playing in a Final Four game, where it actually makes sense to leave it all out on the court because your season might be over tomorrow. For gamblers there's always another tomorrow, no matter how broke or psychologically wounded you might be. *You are playing!*

In my excitement I think I'm still young, but then I look in the mirror and realize I've aged horribly. That's the way this ludicrous life goes. You live a version of Oscar Wilde's novel *The Picture of Dorian Gray* where it's the mind and personality that don't mature, and the body rots at an accelerated pace until you gladly slash the painting to shreds.

Here's something else you might not realize. To the sickos like me, major sporting events are just another day. If we're being brutally honest, Super Bowl Sunday actually annoys compulsive gamblers because fewer overall games are being played, which means less action for us.

It's probably been fifteen years since I cared about the Super Bowl. Which is crazy because I used to do it up right, laying out the spread of chips and dip, three kinds of pizza, grilled burgers, and lots of people coming to the party. Now I spend that afternoon alone like a widow whose kids have grown up and live far, far away. The festive and bustling stage of life has passed, and now I'm just quietly hanging on day by day.

Maybe it's tragic, or maybe just inevitable. Fatigue comes for us all, that world-weariness borne of too many years spent focusing on inconsequential contests happening somewhere else. But instead of religious scholars intensely debating how many angels can dance on the head of a pin, we've allowed our hearts, our fortunes, and our egos to get tangled up in the fruitless pursuit of arbitrary perfection.

Who really cares that you nailed the point spread on one game, if you also lost the five other bets you made on impulse? No matter how much information we've got about the odds, starting rosters, or field conditions, we inevitably chase defeat by placing too many wagers within the same game. Did that late goal really screw you, or did your greed get the better of you because it just wasn't enough to win a couple times already?

The taste of victory doesn't satisfy because now we smell blood in the water and want to devour everything in sight. This is how we fall into the trap and get eaten by a much bigger fish...

I feel a lot of guilt toward my family because they're stand-up people who go about life the right way. I wish I could tell them how I spend my days, but I can't ever bring myself to follow through. I regret so many things that I've done because it's all been predicated on me. I'm just totally selfish. I want to be in action. I want to do what Joel wants.

I've hurt a lot of other people along the way as well.

It's a hard life. It wears on you and beats you down. You keep making poor decisions year after year.

I have a recurring nightmare about how it all ends for me. A news report on TV says that my body was discovered in an alley or floating in a waterway. Sometimes it's murder, sometimes it's suicide. The point is, that's how my family finds out about my death. They later learn that I never got the gambling under control and had been deceiving them the whole time. Meaning that in the world of this dream, I never got serious, never learned self-control, and now I'm dead. Gone forever with everything important left unsaid.

The pain lingers after I wake up, and yet I still cannot stop gambling. It's like being conscious while under anesthesia, where you feel every surgical slice and clamp but are powerless to scream for the torture to stop. This is my reality every hour of every day.

Now do you understand why people who know they need help sometimes can't actually take the steps to get it? We would give anything to have the healthy and prosperous life that everyone else seems to take for granted.

4. THE CURE FOR BOREDOM

Life can be really boring, you know? And so aggravating, too. Getting stuck in traffic, dealing with endless paperwork, your dishwasher breaking down, it goes on and on.

Now considering all the hype about heroes we find in myths, fairy tales, and blockbuster movies, I've got to ask, where can your average person be great in the modern world? Sure, the TV commercials will pander to baristas and long-haul truckers, but let's be honest, our culture is mostly just everybody trying to sell each other on something.

Sell your coffee, sell your beer. Sell that dress, sell those jeans. Sell yourself as a spokesperson for someone else's brand. Sell your travel lifestyle and call yourself an influencer. And hey, why not sell your ass and pictures of it, too?

But none of that is why *I* sell. I love sales because it means each new day is a blank canvas. You never know who you're going to meet or how much money you could make. The sky's the limit!

Every lead is a chance to make a connection with someone cool, someone unique, someone else who's itching to break out of the routine that's boring us to tears. Nobody knows how it happened, and we're all in a bit of a daze, but the world seems to have gotten stale and overly cautious.

So maybe I'm not just looking for thrills, but a way to recapture the feeling of what life in America used to be about. It was hopeful, it was fearless, and you felt free! You got to live your life and let the chips fall where they may without some mob hounding you over your carbon footprint, or because some joke you told at a party made the rounds on social media and now you're the internet villain of the week.

That's why I think maybe sales and gambling go hand in hand. First, you've got the intimacy of the moment – do you close the business, do you win the hand? Then there's the potential for great gains – another job working on your craft, or making that life-changing money. But there's also the risk of failure and disappointment which you have to learn to fight through. Maybe you go broke for the umpteenth time and discover a new way to come up with the money you need to play again, by hook or by crook.

When it's just you face to face with a potential customer or the other last man standing in a poker tournament, I tell you, that's living! You're truly free even as your fate hangs in the balance. That's the moment where everything's electric. You don't know what's going to happen next, but the important thing is you're in the mix. You've got some skin in the game, no matter how high the stakes or how shady the venue.

Compare that to everyone who walked the straight and narrow all their lives. Like those working in insurance, collecting a steady tithing from the other people who are so worried about the unexpected jostling their boat. Or diligently funneling money into conservative stock portfolios year after year – content to *slowly accrue* their nest egg for a retirement that's decades away.

No, thanks! I'm here to hit my version of a buzzer-beating 3-pointer every damn week! Close that $25,000 irrigation contract in the afternoon, then let it ride betting the under on the Jazz-Hawks game. You gotta play... and play to win!

The thrills and the danger, they really are the cure for boredom. Sure, sometimes your impulsive actions might set you on the path to indentured servitude or even committing crimes you're really not wired for, but at least it's *something* more than the endless cycle of paying bills, vacuuming, and shopping for groceries.

The gambler's life really is a war against boredom and boring people. If you've ever fudged the numbers on your tax return, or sped down the highway after a few beers, ever done anything *they* said you shouldn't do...

Then you're in league with us gamblers. On the side of... well, maybe not *good*, but it's definitely the opposite of all those schoolmarms and bureaucrats who sit on their lofty perches and tell everyone *no*.

Meanwhile they go about their empty lives upholding all the rules, and not for some noble reason like defending civilization from marauding barbarians, but because they never had the *courage* to take a single risk. They hide behind their suits and fancy job titles, slowly dying inside.

Credentials versus courage, that's the battle right there. Diplomas versus dice. Control versus chance. Playing it safe versus playing for keeps.

If only the meter maids were so adamant as part of some great philosophical belief system, rather than because they're afraid of living, then *maybe* we would feel a hint of contrition and change our ways. But no, these sticklers are the embodiment of everything about life that we *know* is wrong.

To hell with the hall monitors, because the truth is *no one* is writing the *Iliad* of the twenty-first century behind those gilded doors. They twiddle their thumbs while crafting policy, never once considering the wisdom of pulling their heads out of their asses. Why? Because their existence is purely cerebral, but it's got no brains!

These are the types that try to micromanage every aspect of our lives without knowing what it actually *takes* to get anything done. I bet you not one person working at some fancy think tank in D.C. ever hoisted a 4' x 8' sheet of drywall on a construction site – which is why I don't trust them when they say they want to "change the world."

Just remember, they might be able to get you called out on a technicality, but they'll never swing for the fences when they're up to bat.

Yeah, I may have left a trail of bad decisions in my wake that's a mile long, but at least I made every one of them with total commitment, and full knowledge of the consequences if I failed.

Maybe they ought to put *me* in charge of one of the big cities that are falling apart, 'cause at least I ain't naive. When I say I'm going to do something, I'll see it through to the end.

That's right, Mayor Soper here, reporting for duty! And you know for a fact that my time in office will be *anything* but boring...

5. LAST SECOND LOSER

Final play of a meaningless bowl game. It's already a blowout, the losing team has the ball on their own 20-yard line and they're down by 28 points.

I've got $2,800 riding on the under, meaning that for me to lose they would have to score a miraculous touchdown that has no other impact on the game than flipping the point spread.

And it happens.

One of the wide receivers gets the ball from the running back on an end-around and heaves it to another receiver who's open behind the secondary. He waltzes in for a touchdown with zeroes on the game clock.

One moment I'm planning a night of celebration, the next I'm shaking my head in disbelief. That's when I flip the switch and the rage comes out. I'll shatter a water glass against the dining room wall like a petulant child as my throbbing brain tries to conjure up an aneurysm. The Buddha, I am not!

These shocking turns happen to me time and time

again, and I just don't understand how. It's always in the final seconds of a game that something improbable occurs to cost me a sure winning bet that I've been tracking obsessively.

Is God punishing me for gambling? Does a network of corruption so vast and sophisticated exist where a signal can be sent to one or both of the teams letting them know that a touchdown *must* be scored? Can that many of the coaches and players and referees be in on it, even in college football which is famed for its heart and soul? Or am I the star of some cosmic test, where God controls all the pieces while repeatedly trying to teach me the same lesson until I finally learn and change my ways?

Or is the improbable only permitted to happen during inconsequential games, as if one of their primary functions is to feed the gambling industry? Addicts like me are always getting in on the action, because to *us* there are no meaningless games. Every single one represents a chance to feel the excitement that comes from winning, no matter which team is hitting, throwing, or chasing the ball.

As for the players, I guess a lot of them have their own reasons for going along with the racket. Some are just pragmatic about the ways of the world, others really are corrupt, and others simply happy to play sports for a living rather than working in the factory that makes the basketball hoops they shoot at.

I just don't understand how I can lose *all the time*. I have squandered millions of dollars gambling over the past thirty years – but if it just made sense then I could sleep at night knowing that I did in fact lose fair and square.

Who knows, maybe the rule with professional sports is

that the two teams are allowed to play the game organically until there's an *anticipated* winner, kind of like how all the other cyclists hang back during the final leg of the Tour de France so that the champion gets to bask in his triumph while cruising toward the finish line. And then what? All the guys in the hockey rink know there needs to be two empty-net goals before the end of regulation so that the bookmakers in Vegas can collect from chumps like me? It's mind-boggling.

Is it a global conspiracy or my own personal insanity? Is it just "the price of having sports" in an imperfect world, or is gambling simply one drug among many offered as an opiate for the masses? Am I on to some deep, dark secret or just paranoid?

How come so many of us lifers can't get ahead? We put in the time researching a whole array of factors and statistics before placing our bets, yet time after time we walk away empty-handed on what we thought was a sensible pick.

Seems like everyone's getting paid but us gamblers. From the star point guard to the owner of the dive bar that's only got two small TVs, every link in the chain gets their cut. Apparel manufacturers, corporate sponsors, autographed rookie card sellers, ticket scalpers, hot pretzel vendors, on and on…

They're all making money and enjoying life as satellites in the orbit of a sports franchise. They're out there having a good time and making memories with family and friends.

Meanwhile I'm biting my fingernails down to stumps freaking out over a team whose quarterback's name I don't even know. One time I literally cursed a women's college softball player to hell because she hit a walk-off home run to cost me money. Her childhood dream that was playing out on the diamond had become my own real-life nightmare...

Even when I win, there's not enough true joy in the thrill. All it does is earn me a short reprieve from the hamster wheel of torment. Even the bookie who begrudgingly has to pay up knows that I'll be back tomorrow to throw that money into the bonfire, never to be seen again.

For all the fortunes that we gamblers have lost, nothing is worth more than our loss of innocence. Consider the mystique of fanning out cards over a green-felt poker table or the spectacle of a Saturday Night heavyweight boxing match at Caesars Palace. For us, it's just papier-mâché covering up a festering wound within the soul of humanity, a sick manifestation of the Seven Deadly Sins writ large.

Pride. Greed. Gluttony. Sloth. Lust. Envy. Wrath.

Addiction engorges our worst instincts, tempting and compromising us so that we're unable to stay grounded in real life. Believing that you're better than others without actually having accomplished anything. Hoping to win the lottery and magically get plucked out of your mundane existence, then lounge around like royalty because you've got money in the bank.

But like I say, there's never enough zeroes. A gambler at heart isn't content to walk away from the table and sit on his throne, because what he wants can't be stacked or stockpiled or even counted. It's something he sees dancing in the horizon of his mind's eye to be forever chased.

It's a victory that's quite real, and you'll see it on the face of the World Series of Poker champion and the cheering crowd – but it's also ephemeral and fleeting, like sand running through your fingers on a beach you'll never possess and can't just savor for the day.

It's a taste of immortality, of not staying in your lane and instead punching above your weight class. It's a reckless dream filled with far more sorrow than magic, but without it you're just a little man who really hasn't done that much with your life. You're not content with how you've played the hand God dealt you, and now you'd rather burn two cards and see what fate has hidden inside the rest of the deck.

Which is why we gamblers, when faced with the choice between risking the last few dollars crumpled in our pocket or limping away with an ounce of self-respect, we always say to let it ride.

6. BRING ON THE RAIN

I'll never forget the days I spent at the racetrack back in the '80s. All that action and excitement, it's when I really fell in love with gambling for the first time.

At sixteen years old I wasn't even supposed to be there, but the bookie I worked for had a table inside the clubhouse so naturally I found a way to get myself in.

First I'd ride my BMX bike over to the Clover Lanes bowling alley and park it there across the street from the Detroit Race Course, then crawl through an open window to get into the grandstand. Next I'd have to duck around corners and wait for the security guys to leave their post on some errand before slipping through a couple more doors that took me up to the clubhouse. Man, oh man, was it worth it!

I'd open up that door and immediately the smell of corned beef would hit me. Then I'd wade through a haze of cigar smoke and greet the older guys. They all knew me from the action I ran out in the streets, so they never had a problem with me hanging out.

They had inside tips on some of the races, but since I was underage I had to rely on a guy named Randy to get in on the action. The first bet I ever placed was on a horse named Bring on the Rain, and would you believe it, as the field made that final turn down the track, the sky opened up and it actually started to rain! I was screaming and hollering the whole time… and then my pony actually won. What a feeling! Bring on the rain, indeed.

Another time after I'd won on a tip that Randy had personally given me, he handed me my money and said, "Hey, are you gonna sprinkle the infield?" That meant he wanted a little kickback for his inside information. What could I do, say no and miss out on future bets? So I peeled off twenty bucks and that made him happy.

Those were the days, I'm telling you. An old school cast of characters living the racetrack life and I was there to bask in the glory of it all. I can still see the bookies puffing stogies and drinking whiskey on the rocks, while the crowd below roared as the ponies thundered toward the finish line…

In between races I'd head over to the food table where they kept cooked meat under heat lamps. The chef piled your corned beef sandwich a mile high and you'd savor every bite of that perfect moment in time.

Thirty-five years later and maybe I'm still trying to relive that scene. I suppose too much has changed for that to be possible, though. The track closed down years ago, most of the Detroit guys have passed on, and I've lost too much to find satisfaction in the little perks anymore.

I need the big rush just like junkies crave another hit and extreme athletes jump off of mountaintops with a parachute in their hand. At least they die when they hit rock bottom. Us gamblers? It's an addiction without toxic chemicals or imminent danger. A slow burn of our souls that spans decades. And most of the time no one even notices, unless we end up getting our cars repossessed or a loan shark comes to our workplace to collect an outstanding debt.

But usually we pay back just enough of what we owe while also racking up more losses, and thus they keep us walking in circles on their leash. The truth is, a lot of people behind the scenes rely on us to lose money day in and day out. We fund their vacations, trips which *we* should be taking. We buy their kids' clothes and pay for their college.

No wonder the food doesn't taste so good anymore. You can't compare gourmet sandwiches from an idyllic youthful memory to the reality of what being a gambler looks like after decades of defeat.

I'm not even hanging out in Vegas or at some flashy Indian casino. Instead I'm sitting at a wobbly table inside a seedy Mexican restaurant up in the San Fernando Valley, and using my laptop to place bets on a Costa Rican website. The place operates as a gambling front and the guy who runs it takes my money without even having the decency to comp the cheap burrito I'm eating. Ten thousand a week I've been losing to the guy for years, and never an ounce of sympathy from him, not one dollar of credit.

Cash only, amigo!

I may be sick, but these bookies are *sick*. I can't control myself and I need help, but at least I'm chasing that feeling, the rush that courses through your veins and says you're *alive!*

The bookie with the burritos? He's ice cold. It's all about the money with him, nothing more. Selling crap food, collecting bets… It's pure greed and no soul, let alone any real smarts.

Me, I have to hustle every day to land new customers and close sales in order to get my hands on the money I shuttle up to him three, four times a day. Back and forth I drive like a madman, while he just sits there in that ugly little dive where he runs an illegal sportsbook – the opium den for fools like me who pursue the impossible, one parlay at a time.

I hope he's happy. I hope he sleeps like a baby at night. Because he's the big winner when all is said and done, not me. I've been getting clobbered every day in a thirty-year boxing match against the house – and the house always wins, round after bloody round.

I just wish someone would throw in the towel for me, because the champ seems content with putting on a good show rather than putting me out of my misery. God knows I'll keep running out of the corner head first every time the bell rings to signal a new round.

I may be a loser, but I've got more heart than half the world combined, and I'll never stop throwing haymakers.

7. THE SILENT KILLER

As the bad breaks pile up over time, it starts to destroy you mentally, physically, and emotionally. Lose enough games in the closing seconds and you really think about jumping off a cliff or running into traffic because you just want the pain to be over.

Most compulsive gamblers can only last three to five years before they crumble. Add that trifecta of invisible suffering to all the financial losses and it just eats you alive. That's why so many of us end up dead, in jail, or at the local psych ward.

Because at its core, gambling is about proving that you're right—that *you* know what's going to happen and can control the outcome. So when you're wrong *and* it costs you money, that's a gut punch most people can't handle repeatedly.

I swear, sometimes I'd rather have hot needles poked into my eyes than be a compulsive gambler anymore.

Of all the defeats a man endures in life, gambling losses seem to hurt the worst. When you ask a girl out and she says no, it definitely sucks but you have no idea what's going on in her life. Sure, it dings your pride a bit, but at least you had the balls to approach her. And would you look at that, there's another cute girl right down the street!

If you lose your job for whatever reason, that's also a bummer. But as long as you didn't cost the company ten million dollars or murder one of their clients, chances are you can dust yourself off and find something new across town in no time.

But gambling…

For something that happens so far away and is outside your own sphere of influence, it really does sting more than a girlfriend leaving you for another guy or getting turned down for the position with life-changing prospects. How can that be?!

Because it's not about your heart or your mind or your talents and abilities. It's your own ego walking hand in hand with a *deep need* to be validated.

"I'm so damn smart."

"*I* know what's gonna happen."

"People are going to look at me in awe and say to each other, 'How did he know to make that pick?' "

Well, smart guy, you didn't know. Over and over and over again, you keep picking wrong.

Meanwhile when a scientist finally succeeds after a hundred failed experiments, at least he's got a tangible breakthrough to share with the world and feel good about. Hell, just learning how to play a new instrument or figuring out the assembly instructions on a piece of IKEA furniture is actually doing something.

With gambling all you can hope for is to win the next bet, but if you choose to ignore the feedback loop then that becomes almost impossible. So for me to collect ten grand after losing fifty thousand over the course of a month... I really shouldn't act as insanely happy as I do.

But combine one part goldfish memory, one part living for that moment of glory, and one part being a member of your own religious cult – "Send me your money and God will deliver more miracles than you'll know what to do with!" – and maybe you can see how the monster is created.

Now that we're about fifteen years into the smartphone revolution, some social scientists are coming to the conclusion that people aren't necessarily increasing their knowledge or making better connections with each other. No, putting a device in your hand which can give you everything you ever wanted has actually served to *amplify* the depths of who we really are.

Creative types can use it to quickly record a new musical idea while they're at the grocery store without forgetting it. Financial whizzes make profitable stock trades while sitting in the bleachers at their kid's baseball game.

But for the mentally or spiritually weak, smartphones have the power to turn quirks into perversions and bad habits into cancerous lifestyles.

There's the news junkie caught in the infinite scroll of political warfare on Twitter, but he never actually speaks at city council meetings or organizes a litter cleanup. A middle-aged guy who has a thing for younger women falls into a pit of lust online and ends up getting nabbed during a police sting operation, when in real life he would never be so reckless as to walk up to an adolescent girl.

The smartphone has liberated the gambler from having to get dressed and drive down to the casino, then sit at the poker table like a civilized human being or go through the process of actually pulling the lever on a slot machine. Now he can sit on the couch, or in traffic, or while his children live with the ex-wife, and micromanage dozens of bets like a symphony conductor.

The first period score of the Red Wings versus the Penguins. Second half points in some no-name college basketball game in New Jersey. However granular you want to get, the wager is there to fillet your soul a dozen ways per game.

I really ought to open an old-timey gambling establishment. Call it the Amish Sportsbook. You only get to pick winners and losers versus the spread, and all bets must be placed prior to game time. Then you're free to walk away and enjoy your day out on the golf course, rather than refreshing the screen on your phone like the rat in that old lab experiment.

Because even if you win regularly and make great money, consider what that kind of a life *looks* like! A grown man with a proper education and a successful career madly rubbing your finger against a rectangular piece of plastic like you're trying to give Lady Luck an orgasm...

You know she's a whore who's been leading you and a million other guys on this whole time. When she screams for you and makes it rain, just remember that she's probably faking it and only stroking your ego to keep you coming back for more.

To make another sacrifice at her insatiable altar. To keep your attention focused on her litany of soothing promises, rather than question all the lies you've been telling yourself. She'll be whoever you want her to be and say whatever you want to hear, just so long as you've laid money down on the dream line.

But when the rug gets yanked out from under you in an improbable way with seconds left on the game clock, that's when she slips from your grasp and fades away. Now you're the groom who got stood up in church, choking on bile and wondering how you could have picked so terribly wrong... again.

That's why the life of a compulsive gambler so often crashes and burns into tragedy. You're a living example of the parable of the fool, an embodiment of he who scoffs at the Seven Deadly Sins because you never thought the *deadly* part could catch up to you. Because you were so damn *smart*, you knew how things were going to turn out.

Except I never expected to be standing alone on the Coronado Bridge in San Diego, where one night in January of 2017 I looked down into the water getting ready to jump. My brilliant crystal ball didn't foresee that a bookie so fed up with me not paying him back might send a goon to jam a pistol against my head. And I never knew I would be so willing and able to lie to my own family.

But it's all true, this hell of my own making. The silent killer which is only going to get worse as legalized sports betting spreads from coast to coast. A whole new generation is gleefully marching off to get slaughtered.

In the face of such a bleak reality, maybe I'm writing this book to serve as a lifeline both for myself and everyone else who's caught in the whirlpool of gambling addiction.

Surely some of us deserve a chance to escape and redeem ourselves.

8. THE DROWNING MAN

Nobody wants to help a drowning man. But they'll stand on the shore and watch him struggle to his last breath and sink to the bottom of the ocean.

What I see happening in society is even worse, because we're all drowning in something – our pain, our loneliness, our addictions – and we look at each other like vultures gleefully preparing to devour a fresh carcass.

I am a compulsive gambler and I can't help myself. I know that I'm sick. So how can it be that I'm left to my own devices to not only squander millions of dollars, but also put my very existence at risk through this dangerous lifestyle?

If you owe a bookie a lot of money and can't pay him back, he might just send someone over to kill you because you're better off dead than being a constant headache. Plenty of gambling addicts end up committing suicide when the years of agonizing losses catch up to them – when their souls simply can't bear the collective weight of all that torment caused by their own terrible decisions.

I'm sure that the people who work where I gamble laugh at me behind my back and call me a loser. But they'll never say no when I hold out a dollar that I want to bet. They might be standing behind the counter of some business rather than on a blighted street corner, but they're all still drug pushers in this microcosm of fleeting dreams.

I've had a social worker throw her hands up and say that I was "constitutionally incapable" of being rehabilitated. She thought I represented the worst-case example of gambling addiction. In her eyes, I was incorrigible and irredeemable.

Even her colleague, who had spent years in prison himself, once told me, "You're sick. We can't help you here." Can you believe that? What if someone had said that to *him* before he cleaned up his act?

Four years and over a million dollars in losses later, I'm still out there flailing in the water without a single person sparing a word of concern, let alone offering to rescue me. Not one lifeguard put down their binoculars to dash across the sand, fight through the waves, and haul me back to dry land. No Coast Guard boat responded to my cries of mayday and turned in my direction. Nobody on the pier overlooking the surf could be bothered to toss down a rope or life ring from their idyllic perch.

I know that this lifestyle will end badly for me. I also know that I'm not alone. So rather than disappearing into nothingness away from the world's apathy and contempt, I'm going to leap out of the water like some great whale and flop onto the surface, so that all the other gamblers being devoured by this affliction can grab hold for dear life.

Yes, I, perhaps the worst gambler of the past quarter

century, am baring my soul in this book so that I might help save other people's lives. I don't claim to be qualified or know where we're going, but all the charities and government clinics haven't stopped us from falling through the cracks, so I guess it's on our shoulders to find a new way to resist this curse.

Maybe it's righteous anger that we need as fuel. Anger toward everyone who knows and chooses to look away... those whose job it is to help addicts but still gave up on us... and finally, all the intermediaries who facilitated our downfall every step of the way – including the officials in government and law enforcement who let the illegal rackets ensnare their weakest constituents.

Not that legalized gambling is going to make things any better. I recently saw that flashy commercial with Jamie Foxx shilling for MGM's new sportsbook and it made me physically ill. The gambling industry is using all the Hollywood tricks to rope in a fresh crop of suckers, while also removing the obstacles that guys like me put up with for years by betting on offshore websites.

It's just one more tax in a society that sells the illusion of participation. *Get in on the action while watching the big game!* Just another tantalizing thrill for those willing to grab the shovel and dig themselves deeper into the hole. One more minor distraction that further clouds your mind while offering the promise to be part of something.

But the cost is too high in every sense of the word. First, you lose your love of the game. You care less about your favorite team, or sometimes root for your most hated rivals' players. The score at halftime matters for the wrong reasons and turnovers late in the game seem very suspicious when the resulting score flips the over-under in a flash.

You become angrily paranoid about conspiracies – all because one day years ago you innocently decided to complicate your enjoyment of sports by putting your own hard-earned money on a line that you couldn't influence.

Yup, you voluntarily jumped into those churning waters which are now trying to drag you down. Maybe you just casually waded out there and then woke up to find yourself caught in an undertow. The point is, you're adrift while the world's callous judgment proclaims that it's your own damn fault. They say it serves you right if you die miserably.

Which is so perplexing and ironic because normally the world is forgiving of so much. Society will offer excuses and bend over backwards to overlook some of the most brazen corruption and violent criminality known to man. But don't you dare be weak! Don't admit that you're powerless and need a helping hand!

They'll make a big groveling show of forgiving the aggressor, but not someone who's all too human. Why? Because they see themselves in that mirror, and it scares the hell out of them. They'd rather try to rehabilitate a monster and risk getting mauled to death than stand alone knowing they're just as capable of choosing poorly as you.

We gamblers lead ourselves into temptation, coaxed by unrealistic fantasies to enter the valley of sin and death where we overshoot our mark by a mile. We live out the passion play of timeless human foibles as we reach for the glitz and the glamour, forever desperate for a first-class ticket on the express train which promises escape from the humdrum life.

Everybody wants that *deus ex machina* to save them. They'd be crazy not to scoff at the roadkill that tried and failed.

"He probably brought it on himself."

"Not unlucky, just stupid! But *I* know better."

They toss their cigarette butts over the railing and head back inside the riverboat, retaking their seats at the gaming table as our bodies whip and swirl around the murky waters below…

9. THE DREAM OF ICARUS

There's a girl I've been seeing lately who barely knows a thing about sports. But I'll be damned, she's got a better track record of making picks than me.

Which is of course how we all get hooked. You start with straight bets, graduate to multi-game parlays, then it's quarters of games, and finally real-time wagers. That's the process, like being handed the cement mix to bury yourself.

But with her being so successful as a novice, it's got me wondering what the hell my problem is. I've been gambling for over thirty years and I still can't reliably come out ahead. Is it the sheer number of bets I place that ensures the total losses will be higher than my take? Or am I betting too much money on every play, whereas my girl only puts down twenty bucks at a time?

Maybe it all goes a lot deeper and darker...

It's not just that I do my due diligence before each wager, but the decision itself is solely *mine*. Not only am I known to go against popular opinion, sometimes I'll deliberately ignore a sensible call made by someone who doesn't even gamble. Afterward I'll tell them, "I should have listened to your advice."

Then I have to ask, is it even about sports or money or the action at all? Could it really be just about me? What am I trying to prove to the world? That *I've* got to be right. *I've* got to be the winner. *I* need to be the one who did it completely on my own.

And if that's not a flavor straight out of the Old Testament, I don't know what is. Man's pride and hubris flaunting in defiance of God. While the elation I feel after the occasional win is in fact godlike, on the flip side I often blame God for causing me to lose.

But what would you have me do? Renounce all worldly possessions and move to a kibbutz in Israel? Believe me, I was able to gamble away over $400,000 while living at a halfway house under strict supervision, so even a commune without electricity probably wouldn't stop me from finding trouble.

No, I've got to stay in the gladiator arena of my own making and fight these demons. I need to crack the code on how I routinely lose over 90% of my bets. Maybe I'll run an experiment one day where I put half my money on all the picks I *don't* want and see what happens.

Because really, this streak of bad luck is bigger than me. I am far from the only person who's gone maddeningly broke after years of gambling failure. If I can figure this out, it could lead to the liberation and possible enrichment of not just myself, but also many others who are overdue for a place in the sun.

So… What do the bookies know that we schmucks don't? Which aspects of human psychology are the big casinos privy to so that the lights keep flashing and the showgirls dance all night at our expense? How do these shady bastards know the exact hooks and lures to put on the line to catch us every damn time?

'Cause it sure ain't luck, I'll tell you that. I wouldn't even call it skill, either. No, what they've got going is more like a science. The fine art of getting a man's hopes up unrealistically, letting him soar too high like the mythological Greek character Icarus… and then watching dispassionately as he plunges to his death.

They cut off his wings and mount them on the wall proudly. Just another sucker who dared to dream big and got taught a lesson about reality.

As more and more states legalize gambling, and sports betting in particular, I keep warning people that a wave of addiction is about to sweep across the nation which might make marijuana pale in comparison. I'm terrified for people because I've already experienced the ravages of in-game betting ever since it first became an option starting around 2014.

Until recently you still had to jump through some hoops to get your fix, but now anyone can be in action all day, every day. You could literally gamble from the time you wake up until you go to bed if you wanted to, and once you get caught in that vicious cycle, it's almost impossible to break free. You're microdosing on any at-bat of any inning of any baseball game. It's a quick, cheap, and easy high – but no one wants to think about the potential crash afterward.

The gambling industry is going to absolutely feast upon the younger generations by offering them all kinds of little perks for installing the apps on their phones. It'll be just like when credit card companies set up tables on college campuses and give out free t-shirts or folding chairs when you sign up for an account. How many hundreds of thousands of students have been bamboozled into handing over their Social Security numbers and then racking up debt with obscene interest rates because of that little tease?

More importantly, who allowed Visa and MasterCard to prey on our best and brightest while they're trying to get a university degree? Who thought it was okay to risk economically crippling students whose only "crime" was youthful innocence and financial illiteracy?

That's why I'm so adamant about raising the alarm about this next big wave of enslavement that's on the horizon. While I may have single-handedly contributed a cool five million to the gambling industry's coffers, perhaps now is my chance to prevent another ten, twenty, or even a hundred million more from going over the falls.

Besides, who's better equipped to take these vipers on than me? I've played every game, made every type of bet, tried all the angles... and still lost consistently. The bookies *love* me and my action. But at long last, maybe they'll finally get a nasty taste of my *reaction*.

You might say I'm the gambling version of the video game addicts who immerse themselves in marathon sessions of those epic online competitions. And just like their stylized avatars which die and respawn hundreds of times while running around the virtual war zones and alien worlds, I too am battle tested and know the terrain intimately. It's time to launch a counterattack against those who masterminded this nationwide invasion!

I will fight them tooth and nail in order to redeem myself, while also shielding the unaware who would be lured into serfdom by these denizens of the modern-day company store.

"Come on out to the ballpark," they say with an ingratiating smile. "Here, take a program. Oh, and by the way, have you had a chance to visit our new sportsbook? Go ahead, place a few bets and take a seat at the bar. Enjoy a craft beer before the game starts… who knows, your whole night could end up being on the house!"

That might sound like a reasonable enough sales pitch, but I assure you this agenda to take gambling mainstream is going to ruin so many people. Just remember, legal doesn't necessarily mean healthy or moral.

It's a cruel and petty world out there, kid. Behind the gloss and shine of the Gingerbread House hides a wicked old crone waiting to carve you up in her kitchen.

I don't know what we're supposed to do in the face of these pressures. Just completely walk away from the magic and mystery of life itself? I'm sorry, but that's too bleak. Besides, if you really want to change your life, you can't be a passenger and expect to grow without falling back into old habits.

How can we redirect this hungry energy to bring ourselves closer to what we really want? There's got to be some sort of middle ground where human existence has deep meaning, and it's not just one greedy fish swallowing up another as far as the eye can see.

10. A FRESH START

I'm not proud of it, but my gambling habit had gotten so bad by the time I was in college that I started selling drugs to people in the dorms. It almost cost me everything before my life really even began, which is a good lesson about how just dipping your toe into something wrong can get you swept out to sea.

In the case of narcotics, it doesn't just attract people with antisocial personalities. There's also plenty of dangerous situations and profitable incentives that could bring out the worst in anyone. Greed can lead to justifying betrayal and even murder, while paranoia might cause you to start mistrusting your own friends and family.

Beyond that, there's a sophisticated legal network that profits off of drug offenders in its own way. What began as a mission to protect society from vice and the ravages of addiction has grown into a very lucrative industry that offers stable careers to a variety of bureaucratic types.

Judges, lawyers, stenographers, bailiffs, and more all

get a nice salary with retirement benefits for doing their part in the War on Drugs. They also get to take part in photo-ops after a big bust or make grandstanding speeches when running for political office.

All made possible by a border they just can't seem to secure after all these decades, not even with ubiquitous surveillance technology that feeds data to the internet in real time. Because everyday people are apparently the actual problem, what with all their imperfections and susceptibility to temptation as psychologists mapped out in great detail last century.

Meanwhile no one seems to be writing inspirational symphonies or doing battle with chunks of raw granite anymore. Instead, half of us are chasing the next high or quick buck, while the rest point at them to highlight their own moral superiority.

Maybe the truth is we're two peas in a pod that represents a civilization in decline. Those lacking in self-restraint find that those who in times past would seek to uplift and guide them, now only look to take advantage of their failings as a steppingstone.

There seems to be no place for wise men in our society because everyone has become some sort of a wise guy. Everybody's scheming and angling while whetting their carnivorous appetites for more, more, more. They want piles of cash, mountains of food, square feet by the thousand... and they've got an armory fully stocked with justifications to get it all without troubling their conscience.

If God no longer exists, it's because the stewards of religion either succumbed to corruption or simply weren't able to keep up with technology's impact on human society. Without God, time also ceases to be relevant –

why delay gratification until tomorrow, let alone for your future grandchildren, when all you desire can be had today for free? Another container ship from China just arrived packed with shiny goodies – the kind of things we used to make here at home – and now all you have to do is find the money to acquire it.

Thus untethered from time and place, we have become spiritual refugees in a world where the infrastructure still functions enough to cater to our needs... for now. Our hedonistic inner animal is let loose to live out the fantasies that pop culture ingrained in us, so let's live it up like it's Las Vegas in 1962, and never mind that we're all huffing on the fumes of a nostalgic Americana memory that's slowly fading away.

That's the *real* drug right there, and the system wants you on it. The crime is to point out that we're stagnating and sinking. They don't want you to see that there's a void, a malaise, a rudderless ship that's going in circles while passengers and crew alike engage in a fruitless orgy of indulgence.

The worst sin is not being immoral or even amoral. It's choosing apathy when you know better – being consciously lazy while loading your cart and kicking the can down the road.

Everything we've imported over the last half century – illegal narcotics, cheap manufactured goods, even all the poor people – stems from the rationalization that we would be *better* and could soar *higher* if just allowed to take a little shortcut. Let someone else do the dirty work and we'll have the time, comfort, and focus to cure disease, conquer the stars, and create artistic wonders.

Anyone who gazes upon our cities without rose-colored glasses will admit to seeing a dystopian hellscape of tent-lined sidewalks, slovenly fools fighting each other at theme parks, sculptures without form, incoherent celebrities, and a government-media complex which glosses over it all with staggeringly transparent lies.

We were not worthy of the supposed great leap forward that globalism promised to bring about. Now it is our job to shake off the hangover of this decades' long binge, take the broom into our uncalloused hands, and start cleaning up the mess of our collective failure.

Otherwise the few who are savvy or ruthless enough to find comfort above the dung heap will have to remain on guard after leaving their gated compounds, because at any moment the hordes might descend to take their lives and treasured possessions away.

I began this chapter by telling you how getting hooked on gambling soon led me to selling illicit substances in order to feed my habit. I ended up getting nabbed as part of a larger dragnet that put away a number of people, including Richard Wershe, Jr., otherwise known as White Boy Rick.

I was in class taking one of my freshman year final exams when the cops showed up and dragged me off to the Kalamazoo jail. I was scared out of my wits because this was the first time I'd ever been in trouble with the law. After being fingerprinted and having my mug shot taken, I spent that night in a holding cell trying not to completely freak out.

The next morning I was transported to Detroit in a police van with another guy who was wanted on suspicion of murder. We passed the time by talking about how bad the Lions football team was. Then I waited another nine or ten hours in a holding cell where one of the inmates kept singing the chorus from that Soul II Soul hit song, "Back to life, back to reality," over and over. It was insane!

Back in those days Michigan had some of the toughest drug-sentencing laws in the country. They were sending first-time offenders away for a decade or more. The charge was conspiracy to possess two to three ounces of cocaine and I was looking at maybe four years in prison. While I had teamed up with two other guys to sell on campus, the authorities wanted my head because I was the one distributing.

On the day of our hearing, my family and all my friends from high school were there in the courtroom gallery. The judge sentenced my accomplices to lifetime probation, then turned towards me.

He said, "And now there's you, Mr. Soper. The ringleader."

My lawyer went up to the front of the courtroom and had a sidebar with him. Turns out he'd done an internship with this judge so they had somewhat of a relationship.

After a few minutes the judge looked at me and said, "Okay, Mr. Soper, we're going to give you lifetime probation as well. You just caught a huge break. But if you so much as sneeze wrong, you'll be going to jail!"

I really did dodge a bullet there. I was just a tiny kid back then, so they would've eaten me alive in prison. But the probation officer I was assigned hated my guts, so she made my life a living hell over the next few years while I finished earning my degree.

After graduation I started working for a lawn care company, and then during one of my regular courthouse visits I learned that she had been transferred to another facility. I ended up hitting it off with the lady who replaced her – turns out we were both huge Detroit sports fans so she and I would go on and on talking about the Pistons, who had their classic championship lineup around that time.

One day she suggested that maybe I should get a fresh start somewhere new. I'd previously told her I had an uncle down in San Diego, and it wasn't long until she approved the paperwork that released me from the confines of the State of Michigan.

I moved to Southern California in the fall of 1994 with a black JanSport backpack, about six grand in my pocket, and a wheel that measures the square footage of people's lawns. I started my first landscaping business by going door to door and introducing myself, built up a huge database with thousands of customers... and the rest is *checkered* history.

We *all* need a fresh start right now. May this memoir shine as a motivational beacon as you begin your own journey toward a more serious, responsible, and grounded future.

11. ADDICTIVE PERSONALITIES

Here's the thing about addictive personalities. It doesn't really matter *what* we want, but we sure do want a lot of it. I know an older lady who's obsessed with shoes, and it's gotten so bad that now she'll even buy new styles in sizes that don't fit her feet! Two hundred pairs and counting for that crazy bird...

I'll share another secret with you that's only revealed by actually living the life, kind of like scratching away the surface of a lottery ticket, hehe. Once you start getting that object of your desire, it doesn't seem to satisfy you as much as you'd envisioned. So then it's on to the next pursuit.

In my case, when I finally get my hands on the money I use it to get my hands on the hookers, who in turn use me to get their drugs. Call it chasing your own tail or thinking the grass is always greener somewhere else, but we addictive types are stuck in a mindset that's especially draining because we happen to live in a permissive society. Everything you crave can be had – for a price.

Money is one thing for sure, but it's hard to take that too seriously when the Federal Reserve can create a trillion dollars with a wave of the magic wand inside their own casino. That cash infusion ends up making its way down to me in the form of asset price inflation. Suddenly the value of my customers' homes goes up by 15%, so what do they care about dropping ten grand of that free money on new piping for their lawn's sprinkler system?

If the money's easy come, easy go, then what's the true source of that energy drain afflicting the addictive personality? I think it's the insatiability of our appetites. One more big win. One more roll in the hay. One more snort of the powder. Always just one more, forever and ever.

Until the next time.

Then we rationalize it away.

"Oh, but I've been so good."

"I didn't gamble for two whole weeks."

"I stayed clean long enough to pass the drug test."

We're like the kindergartner explaining away why he hit some other kid or ripped a poster off the wall. The reason might be ridiculous, but any half-assed excuse is good enough for us because honestly, we don't really care. We don't want to hear it. All this *thinking* is wasting time and keeping us from getting back into the action!

I've got a friend who's a multi-talented creative type. Once he tried to tell me the way out of all this, but I wonder if maybe he really just explained what makes us so different. Anyway, he said that addicts and narcissists always want to *take*, whereas musicians and artists are always *giving* of themselves.

Now what's interesting to me is how there's definitely an intersection where the degenerates and the Bohemians meet, overlap, and mingle, because we're all playing with fire in our own way. But still, my friend makes a good point. I'm all about the mad dash toward something that's outside of me and trying to bring it into my life.

The artist's source of agitation, meanwhile, resides inside of them, and their passion is spent pouring it out through some aesthetic form of expression. Even if their sense of fulfillment is as short-lived as the jackpot winner, at least their fatigue is hard-earned and much more noble than ours.

Which brings me to one of the most crucial questions we must ask ourselves. If you know you're powerless over gambling, how can you make gambling powerless over you? I think this extends to all forms of addiction.

There are both positive incentives and negative repercussions to guide you. You might want to keep that money in your pocket, but if you lack self-discipline then perhaps only the threat of violence or prison will keep you in line.

Accept that you aren't in full command and maybe you can start to reclaim *some* of your power. Relinquishing certain legal or custodial rights might be a bitter pill to swallow, but it could very well save your life. Because chances are, this frantic attempt to maintain a balance means you're just a couple miles from empty. We can't keep going like this forever.

There's no way I'll be able to hustle around town in my work truck drumming up sales when I'm sixty years old. That gives me less than ten years to stop the bleeding and reroute my energy, otherwise I'll probably die of a heart attack before getting to enjoy the fruits of my labor.

It's always easier said than done, because the fantasy is free and tastes like bottomless mimosas on the patio during Sunday brunch. It asks nothing of you, standing there with a gentle smile while lazily waving a palm frond and lulling you to sleep for years and years.

Sweet dreams, Rip van *Win*kle…

Those pleasant visions are oftentimes better than the real thing. Win big and you might just sit there in stunned silence wondering why the victory feels so hollow after all that chasing. When you inevitably lose the money back, in your heart you know that the next prize might need to be twice as large to fill this new void.

The opposite of all this is willpower. It says mean words to you like "no" and "leave". When you're up it tells you to grab your chips and walk away – and when you're down it says told ya so. It might always be right, but definitely not any damn fun. For being a life preserver, this sure doesn't feel like living.

Willpower also implies a goal that's inspired by something greater than the momentary urges of the self. Suddenly your life has more depth, real meaning, and a purposeful direction as you execute on a series of small tasks to achieve a result that might be weeks away – all the while resisting that urge for the dopamine hit which is the price of momentary distraction.

Over time, your whole entity becomes a muscle, a wrapped coil waiting to unleash massive potential energy through something worthwhile. Then you suddenly realize that this little word "no" is about to irrevocably change your life for the better.

Embrace the fact that you're fallible and it's okay to not be perfect all the time. By setting a plan in motion and committing to it, you truly can create a happier future for yourself.

12. HITTING ROCK BOTTOM

As I stand at the precipice of the unknown before making my story public to the world, I can't help but think back on my life the same way I did on that fateful night in January of 2017, when I came so close to ending it all by jumping off the Coronado Bridge in San Diego.

It's a jumble of emotions for me right now – hope, fear, doubt – the same confusing cocktail which seems to have fueled my entire existence and its chaotic pursuit of the highs while clawing away from the lows. Was it all of my own making or have I actually been a passenger this whole time, simply *reacting* to events and urges and stimuli?

I certainly always *did* what I wanted, even if I didn't actually *get* what I thought I wanted. Austerity and holding back were never a part of my nature, that's for sure. So I went after everything that appeared on my radar, sometimes frantically forcing the issue to the point of embarrassment, because I simply had to know.

That first step often set a chain of events into motion

which spread like a wildfire, and I've spent years racing from disaster to disaster while losing the plot as well as myself. There's nothing wrong with dreaming big, but the way I went about it has taken me miles off course – and now my *soul* is exhausted.

I moved to Las Vegas with $2.1 million in my pocket and lost it all within a year. That was money I had earned as an entrepreneur and business owner, mind you, so I appreciated the value more than some oil sheikh or trust fund baby. But for all my accomplishments as a salesman, I waltzed into Sin City as naive as the small-town girls with big dreams who ended up cavorting in the sheets with anonymous Johns like me after the sun went down...

I had aspirations of becoming the world's best sports handicapper. I was going to be famous and retire in the desert, because everybody in the world knew that my consulting business always made great picks. We definitely got clients and brought in some good money, but the problem was that it could never keep pace with my own extravagant ways.

From the start I lived it up thinking I was reenacting a scene from the movie *Casino*, always ignoring that daily drip from the leak in my bank account. You need discipline to make it in Vegas, but I was just having too much fun living out the fantasy 24-7. While a lot of the people I squared off against at the tables were on *vacation*, like Peter Pan I truly believed this lifestyle could go on forever.

It just didn't cross my mind that the money could run out. What can I say? Moderation was never my strong suit, so the dream ended real quick.

Even when I was forced to downgrade from my villa at the Wynn to a shabby apartment in downtown Las Vegas,

I refused to even *look* at the situation honestly, let alone believe that I might fail. Because I'm special, don't ya know? Tragedy only strikes other people… not me!

Maybe it's a blessing we can't predict what God has in store for us. This form of ignorance allows us to seize and savor the present moment, whereas if we could see the pain that lay on the horizon, maybe some of us would never get out of bed.

So there I was in Vegas, cruising down the escalator of defeat and completely oblivious to the downfall I was courting with every careless move. There were so many action-packed days and nights, dramatic showdowns against other gamblers where I'd wager thousands of dollars per hand. Then all the games and the picks, the gourmet meals and comped drinks, and of course that revolving door of women who fulfilled my every desire…

Lots of great memories in there, to be sure. They seem so fleeting now, with the best highlights reduced to a flicker in my mind's eye. I know that the cost was too high, even if I can't accept it. Those moments are what I'm addicted to and I seek them out every day – the price of admission doesn't matter to me in dollar terms.

What's crazy about my time in Vegas is how possessed I was. I never went out to the pool deck to relax, never caught any of the Broadway shows. No one from San Diego visited me and I didn't make any real friends, either. I was just focused on gambling, hustling for clients, and partying with the girls. That was all I needed. I was in my heyday.

I just never could have imagined how awful things would get in the years to come. You have to realize that when I sold my business, that was like being crowned king – it proved to me not only was my life charmed, but my instincts were correct! Defeat from that point on seemed impossible, so when it came and came so rapidly, only then did I realize how weak my exposed flank truly was.

The fact is that I was never fully prepared for the complexities of life. I milked my one true talent, this gift of gab, into earning mountains of cash which I *thought* would protect me. Maybe money can shield you from the worst of what's out *there*, but it sure as hell can't save you from yourself – especially when you're as headstrong as I am.

So when I crapped out in Vegas and had to limp back to San Diego, I didn't pause for any of that overwrought self-reflection you see on the daytime talk shows. I was beaten down and humiliated, but not chastened. Just like today, where an extended losing streak has me convinced that I'm *due* to go on a roll, all I could think of was how to win everything back after having fed my millions to the unquenchable vipers of that desert oasis.

The one thing every experienced gambler knows, even if he can't actually control himself, is that *no one* mops up their bloody trail of losses in one fell swoop. The cascade of disasters that accompanied my return to Southern California might seem like something out of a movie, but I lived them all. How I survived to tell the tale is a miracle.

My first move after getting back to San Diego was to call on some of my former customers and line up new jobs. I needed money to gamble, so I collected tens of thousands of dollars in deposits from them with no intention of completing the work. By doing this, I committed the businessman's cardinal sin, which in turn sent terrible karma out into the universe.

I also racked up such enormous debts with my bookies that they sent their goons over to collect. One guy put a gun to my head and demanded payment. Another punched me in the face so hard that I went flying and broke my ribs against the corner of a table. There were countless times when they knocked on my door and I pretended not to be home, just shaking in my boots while hiding behind the couch.

All this and I didn't quit gambling.

All this and I was still far from hitting rock bottom.

One day in December of 2016 I was taking two of my dogs to the groomer when a swarm of cops surrounded my car and then hauled me off to jail. I spent the worst New Year's Eve of my life in the company of career criminals. When I got bailed out by my sister who lives back in Michigan, I ended up catching a ride with another jailbird whose house turned out to be a drug den full of junkies!

That was the moment I'd finally had enough of all the pain that life had shoveled on top of me. I owed a lot of money on the street to some very shady people, and now with the added prospect of maybe going to prison, this crisis seemed bereft of any silver lining. I was exhausted and mental stress had taken me to the breaking point – it was the culmination of years and years of brutal devastation. I just didn't see any reason to keep on living.

I left that crack house in the middle of the night and just started walking. I ended up halfway across the Coronado Bridge and stared down into those black waters ready to end at all.

As morning broke and the police tried to talk me back from the edge, I thought of my family and what my suicide would do to them. After three hours with traffic stopped in both directions, I chose life.

But even then, despite that wonderful moment of salvation, my downfall was just getting started. The cops handed me over to a team of waiting paramedics who then whisked me straight to the local loony bin. The staff there drugged me up with schizo meds and I soon found myself in a cavernous room surrounded by babbling and drooling lunatics. I felt like I was on acid, constantly hallucinating and crawling out of my skin as a parade of bizarre visions tormented my mind.

After a few days lost in a chemically induced stupor, I noticed a small window of time where security was lax between shift changes – so I slipped through an unguarded door and made my escape! I hustled across the grounds and clawed my way over the fence to freedom.

Whoever was on the road that day must have freaked out when they saw a man wearing pajamas and a robe dashing down the sidewalk in a panicked mania, but that was me. It felt like I ran for miles and miles because there was nothing around the facility.

Finally I ended up at a Subway restaurant. I went inside and asked for a water cup, then bummed a quarter for the payphone. I called a friend and a little while later he picked me up.

And yet, even that nightmare experience was far from the end of my troubles…

I was facing several years in prison for embezzling money from my former customers. Only by the miracle of personal connections was I able to avoid hard time by checking myself into Beit T'Shuvah, a Jewish halfway house located in West Los Angeles. I lived there for a year, attending workshops designed to connect us with our heritage and improve our behavior, as well as working a very humbling job at a pizza joint down the street.

I have to admit that I still gambled the entire time to the tune of almost half a million dollars, despite the risk of being shipped off to prison if I got caught. Why would I do that? Because when you think you're living a charmed life, then naturally you know better than everyone else. Even the people who devote their lives to helping sad sacks like you. Even God.

But *He* knew what I still had coming to me, because I was anything but rehabilitated when I left the halfway house, despite the best efforts of its dedicated staff.

My family was so thankful that I had gotten myself back into the real world that they put a down payment and first month's rent on an apartment in the Palms area of Los Angeles. What did my sick mind do? I figured that if I took on a roommate I'd have extra money each month to place more bets, so I put an ad for the room on Craigslist.

After the first person cut me a check for $2,800, a light bulb went off in my head – I could just keep doing that! So I started taking deposits from anyone who liked the apartment. My goal was to take that money, gamble it and win, then pay everybody back with the excuse that the apartment was already filled. That obviously didn't happen and I kept losing bets.

My mind was so far gone that it didn't even occur to me that something might go wrong, such as when half a dozen people showed up at my place on move-in day, only to find that they had nowhere to live! The cops were called and I was arrested once again, although they ended up having to let me go because my "crime" was only civil in nature. But here's the kicker. When they dropped me off back at home, the officers told all of my furious would-be roommates that if they so much as laid a finger on me, *they* would be the ones going to jail for assault.

In the end, only a couple of these jilted renters took me to small claims court, so again I didn't really learn my lesson. Siphoning money from people is what you do when you're a degenerate gambler – we lie and steal to feed the habit, even if our professed *intention* isn't so blatantly criminal.

That apartment experience did put enough of a scare into me that I thought it might be a good idea to move back to my old stomping grounds in San Diego. I got in touch with one of my former business rivals down there, a guy who knew all about my legendary salesmanship skills, and we agreed to partner up.

Talk about personality disorders, this character was ten times worse than me! After a few months of working together, he one day announced that he needed to withhold some of my pay because winter can be slow in the lawn care business. I told him to give me my money or else I'd leave and start my own competing company.

He didn't like that one bit and proceeded to hack into my laptop computer. Next thing I know, he's posting my name and picture all over the internet while making outrageous accusations about me.

I had to rely on a lawyer I knew to resolve that debacle, then another friend lent me some cash for a train ticket back to Los Angeles. Now I had no money, no car, no ideas, no place to go – and my mind was completely shattered. All the stress and strain of the past five years had crashed over me like a tidal wave and I was truly defeated. I had finally reached rock bottom.

I was homeless for the first time in my life. Me, the guy who could generate a ten-thousand-dollar sale in the blink of an eye, now without two nickels to my name.

I just started wandering around Culver City. I ended up in a park and sat down on one of the benches, then closed my eyes. I'd fall in and out of sleep, and any little noise would wake me up with a terrifying jolt. I was cold, hungry, and scared. At that point I was almost ready to throw in the towel and call my parents to have them help me move back to Michigan. But I didn't, because something told me I needed to stay in California.

That first night in the park was one of the hardest in my life. Jail had been pretty brutal, but the feeling of complete isolation while out in the elements eats at you with its own brand of humiliating dread.

There were some other people who had set up shop in the park and they seemed to like the lifestyle, but not me. They gave me a couple blankets to keep myself warm on the bench that I called home.

To survive I'd help myself to free bites at the grocery store salad bar, or tell the cashier at a fast food joint that they'd messed up my order the previous day and I wanted a replacement. By this time I was looking pretty rough, but I guess the fact I could speak clearly helped me get by.

I befriended a young kid with an acoustic guitar named Jay. He'd moved to LA from South Carolina to pursue the dream of becoming successful in the entertainment business, but soon got hooked on crystal meth and wound up on the streets. I'd sit there listening to him sing and play, not even comprehending the reality of our situation. I wasn't thinking clearly because I could barely sleep. It was a really sad time that's still hard to believe I actually went through.

On the third day, I finally remembered that one of the

guys at the halfway house had mentioned there was a Chabad near UCLA which offered shelter to people from the Jewish community who were down on their luck. I made the long five-mile walk over there on a hope and a prayer. Rabbi Shalom told me that if I came back the next day to do minyan, they'd let me crash on the floor of the temple chamber until a bed opened up.

That night in the park I didn't sleep a wink because I was so excited. I was in desperate need of shelter from the world and a chance to both rest and reset. By the grace of God, that sanctuary provided the safety and sense of calm that I truly needed. I lived there for an entire year and slowly healed myself from the inside out.

That place is the reason I'm here today. Everything I've built and rebuilt stems from the protection and encouragement I found inside the Chabad House of UCLA. The power of prayer is real!

I still gamble. I still throw tantrums and break the occasional cell phone. I may not be fully reformed or in control of myself, but I'm miles above the rock bottom I had sunk to when I crossed the temple threshold and slept underneath its beautiful stained glass windows for the first time.

As I strive to be a better person and worthy of this second chance at life, it is my deepest wish that the book in your hands helps pay some of that goodwill forward to fellow lost souls who are also in need.

13. SUPERSTITION

What's wrong with being superstitious? Nothing about the how or why of losing makes any sense. So whenever we actually start winning, of course we're going to try to keep it going, no matter what *it* is.

I once won a large bet while I was in the middle of taking a crap, so you know what I did? I stayed in that bathroom for the rest of the day – and when I finally exited the throne, I was strutting like a rooster because I had an extra eight thousand dollars to my name. So you see, being *pooperstitious* really paid off!

There was a guy I knew named Noah who was kind of a rolling stone, always bouncing around from city to city and job to job. I let him stay at my place for a while, and I swear to God sometimes he was my good luck charm when it came to gambling.

I actually started paying him to sit on the couch while the games were going. I'd bring him beers, food, anything he needed to stay comfortable and not move from that one spot.

I hate to say it, but I even brought him empty water

bottles to pee in and then dutifully took them away. Oh, well. Any gambler will tell you that after losing your first million, it's a lot easier to leave your self-respect at the door in service of the greater good.

'Cause when we get on a roll, that's the ultimate high. Being in the zone. There's nothing like it in the world, so you'd be a fool to do anything that might make Lady Luck change her mind.

Sometimes you'll wear the same clothes for a week straight. Or not shower for three days. Or eat the same meal over and over. I remember I once ate about twenty-five bowls of Smart Start cereal in a row before my hot streak finally ended. There's a lot of fiber in those oats, but at least I didn't have to stay holed up in the commode during that particular run...

I also tend to be very selective about answering the phone when I'm hot. Some people are just bad luck. And unfortunately, one of them happens to be my mother!

She'll call while the games are on and I'm completely out of my mind. I'll scream at her to stop bothering me and then hang up the phone. She'll try again but I just let it ring. Finally I'll call her back after I'm done betting, but to this day I've never told her why.

So as you can see, the emotional swings of the gambling life bring out the best and worst of us in a big way. When I'm in the green, I can be as magnanimous as a nineteenth-century aristocrat. I'll hand thousands of dollars to people I like – because hey, let's make it rain for everyone, right?

But if I'm down, watch out. The dark side of the human psyche which we all keep hidden behind the veneer of civilization now bares its teeth. The inner monster, so full of greed and rage, who just might go on a rampage if the dice don't fall in our favor.

A lot of people come to bad endings on days that start out just like any other. They wake up in a good mood with a few bucks in their pocket and decide to have a go at blackjack or take on the sportsbook. But something happens when they lose that makes it feel different this time. They end up doubling down with money they don't actually have or accuse someone of cheating. Then the devil perks up his ears and asks, "Mind if I play?"

Now the dangerous spiral has begun. You're in the fight of your life, taking bold chances which could make or break the next few years of your life. After tonight, it's either Bentleys or bankruptcy, penthouse living or indentured servitude. Never the middle ground, nothing normal or average.

It's all on the line, kind of like when an upstart businessman signs a contract with the big boys. But while that faithful gesture involves some sort of tangible product or end goal, we gamblers offer no justification for our own recklessly courageous moves. We want it all and we want it now, with no patience for architectural blueprints or laying the foundations of a structure that's built to last.

Stack those hundred dollar bills up to the rafters, would you? That's the only kind of engineering feat I want to see.

When we succeed, the sweet release of triumph from all that strain we endure is so great that we almost *have* to let the world know. But what people don't see is the lonely path we take while limping away after our fate has been sealed. Looking down into the abyss from a hotel balcony as that sick feeling ties our stomachs into knots, thinking, "How am I gonna get out of it this time?"

And knowing there's a quick way to escape…

Accept defeat by taking one more loss, a final leap far different from all the leaps of faith that got us into this mess.

The mind says, "You've dug yourself out before. You can get back on your feet again."

It's true, but the type of honesty that accompanies battle fatigue also knows that once you've clawed back to a zero balance, you'll make all the same mistakes again because you're caught in such a vicious cycle.

When you're truly fed up with the mad grind that defines the bulk of your days, then the thrilling moments you've been chasing seem even rarer and duller than before. The vision of that scene where it's all smiles and pats on the back has lost its luster.

Then you look in the mirror at your haggard face and ask, "What have I done with my life?"

Suddenly Aesop's fable "The Tortoise and the Hare," which always seemed like nothing more than a silly story for kids, hits home with crushing impact. *You* are the rabbit. *You* lived off the fumes of your own hype. *You* didn't build or plan. And now some scoundrel has all your money and *he* gets to bask in the glory that should've been yours.

Sometimes that painful realization is enough to inspire a comeback worthy of a *Rocky* film. But when it isn't and you know your heart is running on empty, then you pursue self-destruction as one final spectacle to be the center of attention.

Man Blocks Traffic for Hours During Mental Health Crisis

Two Gunned Down Outside Gentleman's Club

Family of Five Found Slain After Apparent Murder-Suicide

So the next time you see us gamblers hunched over a poker table, our darting eyes blazing with the intensity of a death ray, maybe you'll understand that this passionate energy involves far more than just chasing another pot of gold.

We're also trying to outrun our own mortality as seen in the mirror of the soul.

14. LETTER TO MY YOUNGER SELF

I found an old picture of me with my two dogs who later got "arrested" when the San Diego cops hauled me into jail back in December of 2016.

Dreidel and Menorah. They were my buds. Nothing was ever the same after I got caught embezzling money. I really let them down. Just like I've disappointed so many people through the decades.

Dreidel passed away while I was living at the Jewish Chabad in 2018, and Menorah has been with someone else for the past few years. I hope she's happy.

Looking at the photo again, I don't even recognize myself. That man is fit, tan, youthful... and smiling a smile that's filled with hope for the future. Younger Joel has no idea in that nice moment what's coming. No idea how much he has to be thankful for, nor how much sorrow he would bring upon himself in the years to come.

Ten years is ten years for everyone, but the gray hair and paunch you see on me now don't tell half the story. Especially when you age poorly in Southern California, where the winters are mild and healthy food options abound. My priorities were all wrong, my attention elsewhere, and the ravages of time crept up on me unawares.

It's hard for anyone to accept that sometimes revisiting the past has the power to move them forward, as a six-month commitment to fitness and sunshine would surely do for my overall health. But my personality has *always* been about pushing obsessively toward the next goal, no matter how great the losses or the futility of my quest.

Sometimes I'm like that delusional Black Knight in Monty Python's *Holy Grail* movie, who declares after King Arthur hacks off one of his limbs, "It's just a flesh wound!"

The neutral observer might consider me a caricature or a cautionary tale as the wages of sin manifest in the heart, body, and mind. At this point I'd be crazy to think I've got another decade left in the tank if I keep on at this pace.

I'm battered and bruised. My frame is warped, the balding tires are patched, and the airbags were already deployed several disasters ago. But the acceleration pedal most definitely still works, while the brakes have never been tapped, so it just seems only a matter of time before something gives out and I end up flat on my back – a total loss.

I *cannot* let it end this way. I always thought my life was going to be special, so how did it come to pass that handsome young Joel with the sandy hair and cute pups now shuffles into some disgusting gambling den throughout the day like a drug addict frothing for his next hit?

Where did the time go? Where did *I* go? And where is

this all going?

If I had a time machine I'd take it all back – five, ten, maybe even twenty years' worth. But we are who we are, mere wind-up toys marching toward our destiny and the lessons to be found therein. Or in my case, refusing to learn from those lessons. I'll do the same stupid thing a thousand times expecting – no, *demanding* – a different outcome, because of course I know better.

Clint Eastwood has a great line at the end of the 1973 movie *Magnum Force*, where for the second time he plays the no-nonsense cop "Dirty" Harry Callahan. As the compromised Lieutenant Briggs dies in a fiery car explosion, Eastwood stares into the camera and says, "A man's got to know his limitations."

Is that not something philosophers and religious scholars have also been trying to drill into people's heads since the beginning of time? I just can't help but rage against the idea of prudence because all too often it feels so constricting, and there's such a fine line between recklessness and zest for life.

Ironically, it's the guys who never risk a nickel that end up owning untamed spirits like me. I plow the field while they sit inside shuffling papers all day. I'm starting to suspect at this late hour that I may have been blind to a better way...

Because I personally know a number of very successful people who are also fulfilled in life, including actors and film producers whose projects have grossed hundreds of millions of dollars. My company services the landscaping around their mansions and they tell me their stories. They've got the same fire in the belly that I do, but they're not strung out on heroin or driving beater cars. The key seems to be that they've got an outlet, a plan, and self-control.

I simply don't have the discipline and can't trust myself to correctly make the hundred micro-decisions required of adults each day. Does accepting my limitations mean I have to put myself on the "Britney Spears plan" where I'm legally barred from touching my own money? That's a tough pill to swallow. Pride gets in the way, even when I tell myself that I can sell as well as she sings...

It's just hard to trust a logical plan that's guaranteed to improve your life after spending decades always looking for the angle. Cut enough corners and it's no wonder you find yourself running in circles.

It seems like an addictive personality only has three choices in the end: 1) establish legal terms to maximize positive output while also preventing yourself from committing acts of existential arson; 2) get sent to prison where enforcement is absolute and you create nothing; or 3) just die and pass a silent eternity confined to a rectangular box or brushed-metal urn, unaccomplished and forgotten by all.

A visitor to the cemetery might glance at your tombstone and note in passing, "He died so young," never knowing how tired and tormented you were by the time your ticker finally gave out or you wrapped your brain around a bullet.

The title of this memoir is *Never Enough Zeroes*, but surely there's a limit to the pain or number of defeats we can withstand before trying to derail the train. Clearly there's no pot of gold waiting at the last stop, and even if there were, would *it* contain enough zeroes to repair all the burned bridges or make up for the countless life experiences we've missed out on?

I want to go back and tell the younger version of myself in that photograph a great many things. He looks so naive and innocent, and yet…

By that time, he'd already lost a small fortune gambling. Yes indeed, behind the confident smile *he too* was brooding and scheming about how to make it inside the winner's circle of legendary sports betters.

What he couldn't see was how close to the falls he had come. Just as he didn't realize it still wasn't too late to paddle to the shore rather than dig in and accelerate his downfall.

I may have romanticized that Joel in the picture, but what I saw wasn't a complete fiction either. I could have spared myself a lot of the grief which came raining down after that beautiful moment in time at the beach.

Today I take a very different snapshot of my soul. It's the mile marker of a tired man who keeps finding new ways to crash and burn, now grabbing at gnarled roots and the bones of broken dreams in hopes of at least climbing back to the surface. There I will stand naked under the sun, humble before God and desperate for Him to tell me what to do next.

Please, God. Give me the strength to obey Your commands, because I really don't want to meet You in person just yet.

15. CAUGHT IN A PARADOX

Two hockey goals in less than thirty seconds to win $3,500. Would you take that bet? All I needed was for it *not* to happen and I'd have won. But nope, when the losing team pulls their goalie then the world's best sharpshooters get to feast by padding their stats – and ruin my night.

Just a day earlier I won over eight grand on a football game by calling both the under and the winner – but even that money was gone before my head hit the pillow. Why? Because I gamble like that guy spraying bullets with the Gatling gun in the 1987 movie *Predator*, whereas I should be using a bolt-action rifle with a scope. "One shot, one kill," as Tom Berenger so wisely said six years later in the action gem *Sniper*.

The truth is I actually am a good handicapper when it comes to sports, especially baseball. If I was forced to bet on a single game per day then my track record would be phenomenal. I do all kinds of research, like tracking what the weather will be at game time or who the two starting pitchers are, and that's how I put together a smart play.

But winning clearly isn't enough, because *one* ain't enough. After I've placed the wager on my "due diligence" play, I get antsy to see what else is going on in the sports world – and then I want in!

Soccer in Europe, Aussie rules football Down Under... it really doesn't matter. Someone is always chasing after a ball under the lights somewhere and I feel the need to throw my money at them.

Is it lack of discipline or active self-sabotage? Having no life purpose or some sort of motivational paralysis? There's definitely comfort in this state of perpetual discomfort, always being able to milk the inconsequential woeful tale of bad breaks instead of living with a definitive win or loss after taking a truly courageous leap.

For some reason guys like me would rather rage in the shadows than risk getting KO'd under the spotlights, kind of like porn addicts who spend their hours *watching* other people have sex. It's vicarious thrills with nothing wagered or lost on the surface, but always your time and your soul slipping away in a whisper...

Somewhere in our psyche a calculation was made that deemed any kind of defeat not worth the potential gain that comes with victory – but perhaps we remain blind to a third possibility. The truth is that whenever you take a bold chance, you pave new road for yourself which inevitably will lead to open doors.

Speak to the cute girl at the grocery store and it's a double win, even if she shoots you down. You manned up and fought down your fear, and now you *know* how that what-if actually played out. It's one less grain of sand for that ulcer you're nursing to feast upon.

Sign that commercial lease and now you've committed

yourself to grinding out profit for the business over the next several years. The risks are high and the odds may be stacked against you, but you very well might succeed. You'll grow personally along the way, while most definitely *not* going soft like the person who just thinks about doing something.

One of the biggest secrets in life is that for those who *do*, everything connects as part of your lifelong winning season. You become mentally and physically hardy by actively participating in your work and your hobbies. The time passes quickly in the best sense when you're involved, rather than life simply passing you by. Gains stack contentment upon more gains as the intangible takeaways of each experience weave a rich tapestry of the life well lived.

Which is why those who huddle on the sidelines trying to scheme a sure thing almost always have nothing to show for themselves but a floor littered with torn-up betting slips. They mutter to themselves under stooped shoulders while puffing on a cigarette in front of their apartment building, or lounging at the pool hall where they've wandered to see what's going on.

It's the nebulous tragedy of the man who couldn't decide whether to be a participant or an audience member. He was blind to or just didn't want the kind of direct commitment that being a coach or other type of supporter entails.

Instead he sought personal gain while being *around* the main event – and ended up perverting the game itself by manifesting tangential priorities as fueled by obsessive real-time betting. He corrupted his soul and beamed waves of bad energy out into the world when his own careless wagers were "spoiled" by the noble competitors celebrating a teammate's achievement down on the field an ocean away.

Now the veneer starts to crumble into dust...

All the smiling card dealers in tuxedo shirts and waistcoats. The beautiful blondes flinging rosy red dice down the length of a packed craps table. Frank Sinatra singing a tune while the next free drink is set down beside your dwindling stack of chips...

Once you see this in its raw form, maybe you can finally try to stop. Maybe you'll admit that you were sold on an *experience* straight out of a travel brochure, where you as an addict don't have the capacity to limit yourself to just one Saturday night at the casino complete with dinner, dancing, and a show.

You've distorted the "work hard, play hard" adage so badly that your release looks more like that of a decadent ruler in the final days of a dying empire where everything is gotten on loan. You're gambling on credit. You don't have a wife or a girlfriend so you buy some company for the night – and even then you'll have to pay a pharmaceutical company to help conjure up an erection to complete the charade.

This is how one cowardly act can knock a life of great potential miles off course, and the clever shortcut ensures that you'll never find your way home. It's the paradox of how the minor league ball players who never get called up to the majors live a much more fulfilled life than you, despite the occasional jackpot making your fantasy a reality for a brief while. You won, money rained down from the sky like confetti, the girls squeezed in tight for a photo, and the night raged like a river made of champagne...

The fog hangs thick and low in this gray area that

separates the people who put on the uniform and those who coast in the sweet-smelling air of their wake. It's also populated by the fans who love their local team but try to make a few bucks on the side by selling collectible merchandise. Then there's the casino staff who play a part in the action, each profiting without taking on any risk as they help slice away another layer of skin from the gamblers caught up in the heat of battle...

It's a big free-for-all like the California Gold Rush of 1849, where human flesh and casino chips and moments of triumph are the prize, and so many of us end up shoveled aside as useless dirt. Maybe the smart ones are like the shopkeepers that sold work clothes and supplies to those who panned for gold, always keeping themselves one step removed while filling a practical need for the frenzied prospectors...

But then again, is such opportunism not a hallmark of that schemer who's too afraid to lace up the boxing gloves and jump into the ring? Where does *service* become a sinful religion and *excitement* the path to liberation and deep meaning?

It all gets so tangled that you begin to hate the plodding tortoise and root for the plotting hare after all! Because playing it safe all the time *is* boring and there's something to be said for adding a little style and flair to the daily grind.

That's why it's so damn hard to renounce the gambling lifestyle even when it's a source of constant aggravation. You may not be living your best life, but at least you're living! It sure would save us a lot of grief if there was a way to regulate the intensity like a gas stove, but odds are we'd just move on to something else that lacks any kind of safety net.

Because in an age of total surveillance and mandatory insurance for pretty much everything, the gambler's deepest yearning is for a type of freedom that can't be quantified, filed neatly on a shelf, or protected against.

We'll fly so high you won't even see us, and we'd probably resent you if you tried to break our fall.

16. WINSOMNIA

It's funny. When it gets toward ten or eleven at night, in a weird way I almost hope that I've lost all my money. If there's anything left in my betting account then I can't fall asleep because the adrenaline's still flowing and I want to play. At least when the money's gone I know I can't get to the bookie until the next day, so I'm finally able to rest.

I feel so normal when I wake up after not having gambled during the night, just a whole different vibe to start my day. And then, as soon as I'm ten minutes away from the place where I drop off the money, something starts happening inside me. One second I'm totally calm and laid back, then my heart's pounding and I enter this manic headspace for the rest of the day.

Gambling is just such a rush! In essence it's both your best friend and lover, but also a deadly succubus. You feel so at home when you're in action even as it bleeds you dry.

Sometimes the worst thing that can happen is for you to win a few bucks. It gives you a false sense of hope now that you've gotten that taste. You lose it all back of course, then another stack by the end of the week, but you just keep thinking about how you were up that one time. It's a vicious cycle.

I get so deflated after losing. All my dreams come crashing down and it's back to the reality of having no money. I've broken eight laptops and six cell phones in fits of frustrated anger. Man, do I ever wish Best Buy sold punching bags so I could stop destroying my stuff...

Some days when I'm out of money I play a little mental game called "reverse rooting." I'll cheer for the team that I would have bet *against*, so if they win I won't feel bad about missing out on that wager.

Despite the long droughts, gambling isn't always heartbreak and defeat and terror while being chased by goons. Sometimes you really do win big and then it's the bookie who has to put on a grumpy face and count out your money.

I tell you, when I see that stack of hundreds piling high on the counter, my heart swells up like the Goodyear blimp. What a moment!

My mind becomes this jumble of happy thoughts as I experience total euphoria. Then a vista of possibilities opens up in my imagination – cars, mansions, exotic trips, all of it and more.

While prudence and past experience suggest that I should savor each triumph for what it is, that's not how my mind works. Nope, just one foot inside the winner's circle and I know I'm gonna catch my streak – and it'll never end!

First thing I do after a win is get the party going. Steak dinners, beautiful escorts, upper-crust living or bust! No matter how many days I've spent in the gutter like a pauper, I never forgot how to spend the night like a king...

People who know me will tell you that there's no celebration like the ones I throw. Combine all the energy of a bachelor party, the Super Bowl parade, and the coronation of a new monarch into one – that's how I roll. All hail the Soperman... long may he reign!

I always want to keep it going because I'm so amped up after a huge win that I *really* can't sleep. I'm one part kid in the candy store of life, a puppy at the beach for the first time, and Chippendales dancer armed with a bottle of Viagra.

Yep, that's what it feels like when I've got a case of *winsomnia*.

Savoring every flavor under the sun, soaking up the sweetness of life like a sponge. A Caesar salad for this Caesar-for-a-day. A sizzling steak after triumphing when the stakes were high.

Time ceases to exist after I've won, because who wants to remember all the heartache that came before and is sure to follow? For once I can afford the fantasy and I intend to milk it!

Tonight I'm a king sitting on a throne made of hundred dollar bills, so let's toss a few bundles to pay for the feast and those beautiful buns-for-hire. We'll live it up while indulging all our senses, and when the morning comes let's hope there's a few cents left.

We'll grab coffee and exchange a smile, not knowing when we'll return to the peak, but it'll probably be a while. Until that glorious day we'll have sweet memories to pave over the pain, now let us pray to Lady Luck so that she might shine upon us again.

It ain't over till it's over,
but once again I bet the under.
Please make that all-star miss,
so that my wager isn't a blunder.

When the ball or puck bounces clear,
I'll stack my bucks and give a cheer.
Then call my loyal sidekick Sancho Panza
to join me, Don Juan Quixote, out in the plaza.

We'll ride off in search of adventure,
singing serenades to the lovely Dulcinea.
And as days and nights flow like wine, remember,
Winsomnia is more than a state of mind...

17. LIVING A LIE

There are different circles of hell in the life of a gambler and losing isn't always the worst one. A bet often turns sour in the blink of an eye, and then you're on to the next after shaking off that jolt of defeat.

But lying is something else altogether. Constantly misleading those who love and care about you is breaking their heart – or will break it, whenever they discover your dark secret.

Most of my family lives far away so it's a bit easier to keep the ruse going, but that doesn't do much to alleviate the guilt I feel. I can only imagine what it's like for a father to tuck his kids into bed each night knowing he's throwing their college fund down the drain while betting on games being played by other people's grown-up children.

The problem with lies is that there's no such thing as a one-off. They don't exist as freestanding entities, but instead link arms with all the other lies you have to tell to keep the first one intact. That chain soon gets mighty heavy, what with having to remember all the tales which sprouted like mushrooms after that first big turd you put out into the world. It really gets to be too much to bear.

Sometimes you realize it probably wasn't even worth it. The little lies, at least. Because when you owe half a dozen guys fifty grand each and barely have enough money to pay your rent, then you've got to lay it on thick out of self-preservation. You didn't have the dough to begin with when you placed all those bets, so what's another fib added to the one that enabled you to get in on the action? Now you do it to save your own skin, because losing *isn't* an option.

Lying to people when money isn't involved can actually be a lot tougher because here you're messing with the human heart, which doesn't think in terms of dollars and cents. You could be down to your last breath pleading a loan shark for mercy, but as long as you pull out a wad of cash then all will be forgotten. Hell, they'll even take another bet before the next race begins if you've got a couple bucks left over.

But paying off the people you've disappointed isn't nearly so simple. Trust can only be earned the hard way after it's initially been betrayed. There's no parlay bet at any casino in the world that can magically repair the damage done to a personal relationship tarnished by your dishonesty.

Like most other bad habits, it's not as if an addict can just stop doing something that's detrimental for logical reasons. All the rivers of my life feed into my gambling habit – it takes complete priority at every juncture. I work extra hours at my business to be able to pony up the cash for football Sunday. I tell my parents I'm still clean because that's what they want to hear. I borrow from

Peter to pay Paul to keep the juggling act going – because I just *know* I'm due for that big win.

Call it expediency, rationalizing away bad behavior, or shameless hypocrisy, but the point you have to understand is that the casino is my temple. I bow before the gambling gods and place my tithing on their holy altar, hoping desperately that the offering will be returned tenfold.

Maybe a life of lies is even worse than a life of crime. The illegal act is committed in a direct manner, then you either get away with it or pay the price as the legal system's jaws rip time and money from you.

Meanwhile, insidious lies spread like cancer poisoning your bloodstream. The false tongue burrows painful holes inside your brain, causing your psyche to run down endless corridors in the confusion of trying to keep your story straight.

The liar is a spy without allegiance. His goal constantly changes shape and his enemy is fear. He claims to always know best, projecting an image of outward confidence while stealthily pilfering the fruits of what others have planted.

He believes his mission is supreme, but not enough to publicize it or seek true allies. His mind is utterly fixated on the big score which will bring about the fairy tale "happily ever after." He neither reflects after defeat nor wonders what he will actually do with his life after entering the Promised Land.

The dream is his life and he lives for the dream. It's as simple as that because he's convinced it can be so. He ignores the complications that arise to derail the best-laid plans of others, believing in his heart that they just lacked true faith.

What's loyalty or love in the face of religious fanaticism? *Who* in the world possesses the courage to voluntarily own up to a lie which has bloated into a giant tapeworm that's controlling your entire life?

I swear, if you knew the words that could inspire people to come clean, you would spark such a revolution of atonement that they'd probably grant you sainthood on the spot for achieving a true miracle.

So don't get too self-righteous with me about weakness. We're all tempted to sin when it suits our own agenda.

Taking the path of least resistance.

Believing that what they don't know can't hurt them.

Thinking only God can judge you.

That's right, the catchphrases are as readily available as the lies and excuses themselves. Because people have been lying to each other since the beginning of time, while also trying to fool the face they see in the mirror.

You ask me how I can live with myself? Maybe a part of me is betting that I can keep the lie going long enough so that both of my parents die peacefully of old age before ever finding out the extent to which I haven't changed my ways.

I already disappointed them so badly the first time, when I got into trouble and almost went to prison, that now I'll do almost anything to keep them in the dark. I may be weak and stupid and reckless, but at least I'm not cruel.

I still pray to God that one day I'll hit the ultimate jackpot and finally make good in everyone's eyes.

Until then, Lady Luck seductively whispers her own catchphrase into my ear…

It can happen to you.

18. THE REST OF THE STORY

I've been watching these news reports about gambling addiction on TV and you know what? They're talking about it without actually touching it. Sure, they'll identify the pitfalls, but only from a safe distance.

The type of person they highlight is usually a family man who ends up getting back with his wife and kids at the end of the segment to leave the viewers feeling a sense of optimism. They don't point their camera at the army of unmarried middle-aged guys who are getting put into the wood chipper thanks to gambling. Why? Because it's too dark. It would mean we might actually have to do something as a society to help these people.

Promoting awareness is one thing, but the money train needs to keep on rolling. Game time is 7 o'clock Eastern, 6 pm Central. Place your bets, please.

Everybody wants to eat their cake and have it, too. Or be a barnacle clinging to someone else's excitement. These reporters who spend a year of their lives embedded in the gambling life, you don't think they get caught up in it?

Sorry, but this isn't some boring lab experiment testing the speed of molecular separation or whatever. These news guys are human – and they like being on camera themselves. Yeah, the star of the show and the center of attention, just the same as when you win the big jackpot. Oh, but they're *journalists!* Immersing themselves like anthropologists to get the scoop... and the dirt.

Whatever. I'm sure they mean well. But when you work for a corporate media entity, there's always outside pressures sculpting the story to cater to a specific audience or the general public's sensibilities.

What you aren't seeing is the unvarnished truth. Which is why I'm writing this book. So you'll see how getting caught up in the gambling life can make a Jewish kid from a good family in suburban Michigan do things no one ever could've imagined I was capable of. Not even me.

One time I got myself underwater with a bookie to the tune of $500,000 and he had his goons literally kidnap me. They gave me an impossible choice: extreme violence or a chance to get my debt bound by stealing cash and jewelry from a house they'd cased in a wealthy neighborhood.

We drove over there in a van late at night and parked around the corner. They assured me no one was home, then handed me a house key, small flashlight, a mask, and gloves. I went inside, punched in the alarm code, then wandered around in the dark – no way was I going to risk tripping off any sensors with a light beam! I was so scared that at any second the cops were going to arrive and haul me away.

I went into the office and looked inside the closet like they'd told me, but there was only a locked safe and no loose valuables. That's when I really started to panic! If I didn't bring them *something* I figured they'd probably kill me. Then I caught sight of a ring down on the floor. I grabbed it and ran back to the van as fast as I could.

At first they were furious, saying, "That's all you got?"

I said, "I can't carry a thousand-pound safe by myself."

They calmed down after a while because I did what I said I was going to do. I went in there and brought something back. God bless the owner of that house for dropping the ring – it probably saved my life.

So now you know, in order to cheat death I had to commit felonious breaking and entering! When if I'd just kept my money in my pocket, instead of letting it burn a hole through my reputation, guaranteed I'd be able to afford a place in a gated community as nice as the one I was forced to ransack.

But that's how life goes for a lot of people. All the secrets they keep, it probably explains why their lives aren't where we expect them to be. As if a toxic brew of fears and weaknesses and demons combines to manifest self-defeating attitudes that hold them back, as well as destructive behaviors which set them back years.

How much is any individual person to blame? I don't know. A lot of this seems to be hardwired into our DNA, otherwise books like the Bible and Dante's *Inferno* wouldn't still be so relevant today. But if we know the dangers are baked into the human condition, why the hell do we devote so much of our collective energy to not just enabling predators but actually glorifying them?

For example, when Vegas hires your favorite actor or retired wide receiver to shill for the casinos during the pregame show, that temptation to gamble is damn hard to resist. Look, I get it, personal responsibility and accountability and self-control are all very important factors. But these aren't the Puritan times anymore, either. The stoic stiff upper lip might be an anachronistic trait now that you don't need to know how to survive winter on your own.

We have most certainly gone past the "idle hands are the devil's playthings" stage of existence. We outsource so much – foreign countries manufacture most of what we use, and we bring in foreign *people* to do menial jobs – that there's virtually nothing to keep us grounded or humble.

What do we privileged kings and queens of the twenty-first century do with our affluence and free time? Get into as much trouble as we possibly can, that's what! We watch porn, gamble away our savings, order crap food... all from the comfort of the imported couch we bought on credit.

These vices are all modern-day manifestations of Vlad Dracula and we gleefully invite them in to suck our souls dry.

Watch the drug addict with bleached hair and enormous implants have sex. Risk the rent money on whether or not some basketball team whose logo you don't even like can score 25 points in the third quarter. Gorge yourself on GMO slop that was prepared by an apathetic wage slave who didn't bother to wash his hands before tossing it piping hot onto a Styrofoam container – by the time someone else delivers it to your apartment, both food and plastic will have chemically bonded into one.

Mike Judge was really onto something when he made that movie *Idiocracy*. Less than twenty years later and we're almost there: a barely articulate man sitting on a toilet-equipped recliner sucking on a feeding tube while masturbating in front of a giant television screen.

Talk about losses! My God, this goes way beyond money. We're losing our sense of purpose, community involvement, even the ability to express ideas clearly. Long past are the days spent at the racetrack wearing our best suit and waving our hat in unison with the crowd as the horses rounded the bend.

Nope, just a million guys lost in a stupor trying to get a mere *taste* of all that once was, not yet realizing that the dystopia is already here. The downfall of society happened over the course of several great limps backward, and now we are the surviving remnants. Isolated, alienated, and desperately clinging to those unspoiled memories of watching the hometown squad back when we were kids.

Because now… it's gone, all gone.

Look around and maybe you'll be able to pinpoint a dozen culprits. Too much change that happened too fast on all fronts. Too much new technology without enough time to absorb it or guide it. Too many cultures dumped on top of each other without any unifying purpose. Too little God or religion to help ground us and make sense of what was happening over the last quarter century.

When we turned to the familiar in hopes of getting our bearings back, we found that even sports and music and movies had gone off course. Too much overt political messaging in the arts. Too little actual *playing* in the songs. And we personally failed the test regarding sports – using fantasy football as a gateway drug to sometimes rooting for a sworn enemy to make a few extra bucks.

The truth is that if you hate the Dallas Cowboys in

your heart, then you betray yourself every time you wager a single dollar in their favor.

Where's the journalist telling *that* story? Nowhere! Because there's no time to talk about the human soul when new sportsbooks are being set up inside professional sports stadiums around the country. Whether or not God actually has a plan for your life, rest assured that the gambling industry very much intends to sink its teeth into you.

Because hey, at least now it's legal, right?

19. THE UNTROUBLED CONSCIENCE

In the death throes of a gambling binge turned sour, I find myself asking existential questions from a place of desperation. Why can I never seem to get ahead? What's wrong with my judgment? Why do so many bad things happen *to* me?

Hold on a second...

Did you see what I just did there? I framed the consequences of my choices in a way that makes me the victim of circumstance, rather than asking if defects in my character might be the cause. That's a very sneaky trick which we addicts have employed throughout our lives to manipulate other people and avoid blame. But just like the hedonist who's never satisfied despite having all of his desires fulfilled, so too does the serial evader never progress beyond a certain immature mindset.

While we play-act at martyrdom when things don't go our way, another person might just shrug their shoulders or use the experience as motivation to self-improve. The truth is that much of what we perceive as reality stems from our attitudes and perspectives. With this realization comes both the power and the pathway to change.

Not accepting responsibility for the negative outcomes that befall you as a result of your own actions is as revealing as it is damning. Not only do you remain helpless because you believe that you *are* helpless, you also deny yourself the possibility of growth which can only come from an honest assessment of the situation. No discretion means no course correction. If you're too scared or unwilling to appraise yourself, you'll just keep careening wildly until you crash into a wall.

Despite all the artful dodges and deflections, you do know the truth in your heart. Strip away the thousand rationalizations and empty promises, and you still have the capacity to differentiate between right and wrong. You might lack self-control, but it's not because you're physically unable to act of your own volition. When the shriveled up corpse of your conscience suggests that you stop, you instead choose to stick your fingers in your ears and defiantly shout, "La, la, la, la, la. I can't hear you!"

This might be the hardest part of the healing process – to call ourselves to task without throwing a tantrum and hiding under a rock. For a group of people that's known to project a lot of confidence, we sure are sensitive about being criticized. In fact, when non-addicts confront us we view it as a strike against *them*, and discount their advice because they can't relate to what we're going through.

That's the kind of circular logic fearful zealots employ to defend their castle as it sinks deeper into the swamp. As always we *know* better, even while the people trying to save us *live* better.

Oh, well. We don't want to be like them anyway. They're so boring. Stability is the soul killer! Never mind that the life we're racing toward is usually a mirage, because sometimes the chase really is what it's all about. And if artists are allowed to drive themselves insane while trying to bring their imaginative visions to life, then why can't *we* say the hell with the 9-to-5 drag and go for it, too?

The problem is that in our yearning for freedom, we always end up taking things too far. We need what we dread, which is to be completely alone and without the distractions that get us into so much trouble. But left to our own devices – even while denied the electronic devices themselves – that's when we really turn into a mess.

We're antsy, frustrated, chomping at the bit to jump into life! Normally that wouldn't be a bad thing, but the way we run roughshod over everything and everyone to possess that which catches our fancy – it's the kind of behavior that used to get people killed for the sake of common decency, if not the very survival of an entire community.

That's why our confessions ring so hollow. Real people can see through a scripted performance that has no heart in it from a mile away. We're annoyed that we got caught, not genuinely sorry – and everyone knows it. Simply having good intentions isn't enough when it just whitewashes our indifference to the pain we've caused.

A society that's too lenient for its own good puts up with us and we kick them in the shins for their troubles. The world that coddles us deserves so much better, but if they ever actually lash out we put on an offended air and mentally shut down.

Can you guess why? Try this on for size.

You want to enjoy all the benefits of civilization

without being bound by the rules that keep it going. You want to be a star at the center of the stage without having personally shined – and despite the fact you were willing to cut the line, you'd swear on your mother's grave that someone doctored the footage of you sneaking in.

The final boss is the first lie you told that went unaddressed. That evil seed grew into a poisonous tree which saps all life and blocks out the sun. This monstrosity needs to come down if there's any chance of redeeming your soul, but after so many years perhaps your essence has become permanently embedded within its tainted fibers.

Do we really want to change? Or is our wish that night won't follow day? There *are* video game versions of all your casino favorites which you could play without ever losing a dollar. We retort that there's no point without any risk involved, but have we not already proven our willingness to run headlong into the bloodstained arena a thousand times before?

Let's face it, you can't win your way back to even and society's patience is running mighty thin. One by one, the members of your inner circle have withdrawn from the blast crater of your chaotic existence – good people, all of them, whose boundaries you pushed too far.

Your chances at redemption are dwindling as the clock ticks down on a life which you've treated like a game. Are you capable of coming up with a last-second miracle to beat the oddsmakers who are betting that you'll lose one final time?

May this stark message be a lifesaving wake-up call rather than a postmortem which confirms everyone's suspicions. If you're smart enough to understand the stakes then you also have the *ability* to choose a new way forward – even if you lack the actual power to see it through to the end on your own.

But here's a little secret: something magical happens when you allow yourself to let go. A cascade of goodness rushes in to drown out your doubts and sorrows, and soon you're floating on air and drifting away from all those burdens you've been carrying silently for so long.

If you opt for half-measures or vice, just remember there's always someone in the shadows ready to lend an ear or a puff, and years of your life might pass aimlessly in that haze. However, on the path toward liberation you'll meet people whose aim isn't to get their hooks in you. They want you to succeed for your own sake, knowing that behind you winds a long line of others also in need of their help.

It's time to start right now. You never know when your last chance might have arrived.

20. A BETTER TOMORROW

The strategies and rituals themselves don't matter. We've all got our own core belief systems that determine how we bet.

Me, I insist upon taking the under even though nowadays fans want to see a lot of scoring, so I lose pretty much all the time. But I can't shake it, can't change my ways because logic and data have nothing to do with what this is all about.

What *does* matter is that we strike out consistently and don't know when to walk away. Any fun we might've had along the way gets spoiled by the grim reality that we've just added another paycheck to that soaring mountain of lifetime losses.

A person with any sense would take one look and realize that it can never be won back, then leave the table for good. But not us! In our mind, that monstrosity is visual proof of how statistically improbable our losing streak has been and now the odds have *got* to turn in our favor.

The problem isn't what we bet on or that we bet at all. Where we go wrong is *how* and *why* we gamble. If I stuck to only wagering the couple of games I took the time to handicap, most likely I would actually have that name recognition I've been dreaming of. But if there's never enough zeroes, then there's also never enough action to satisfy me – I need to sprinkle a few bucks onto every available pot or will feel like I'm missing out.

What's your poison of preference? Whatever it may be, all I know is the feeling's so right that it almost defines us or expresses who we are, kind of like a person's unique clothing style. That's why it hurts so much when we lose. We ask ourselves, "How can *I* be so wrong?"

Suddenly the pattern we start to recognize has nothing to do with improving our winning percentage, but that our own identity is being called into question. Because if part of what makes you *you* also makes you miserable, and you're truly unable to stop doing it, that's like a stain seeping across the carpet until it risks ruining the whole thing.

The only detox for this type of sickness is spiritual in nature, which you follow through upon by adhering to a set routine. What I mean is, first you have to accept that you got yourself stranded up on Gambler's Peak without food, water, or appropriate clothing, and now the cold of night is approaching. You need to radio for help, otherwise you'll die up there. The good news is that emergency helicopters are standing by – all you have to do is acknowledge that you can't get down on your own and then make that call.

Step two is establishing a new lifestyle to keep yourself from being drawn in to the cycle of bad decisions again. Redirect your focus and energy on *anything* you're interested in that's constructive or at least not counterproductive. Moving sideways can sometimes be a very good thing.

You also need networks of people to call on as a safety net when you get too close to the edge. You should be filling your life with commitments that keep you occupied and mentally engaged. When your hands are full while participating in the game of life, you'll find that some very interesting things start to happen.

Now that you're no longer stealing the copper pipes from inside your own home, what you *have* becomes a baseline on which to plant and build more. You're also working with other people, forming relationships and solving daily problems while infusing your life with a richness that money can't buy – nor be lost in an overtime shootout or after a controversial call by the refs.

It's actually freeing to finally admit that you're not the gambling equivalent of a Roman emperor holding court in a luxurious temple, although the revelation does come with a bit of a downside. As you feel that weight fall from your shoulders and the pit in your stomach slowly dissolves, it's often replaced by a clarity that's almost too sharp and too piercing as you wonder, "How could I have been sucked in by all of this?"

The casinos start to look less like a place of dreams and more like a mousetrap. The purveyors become predators and the payouts a relieving dose of morphine rather than the means to a glorious end.

If you got caught up in the pomp and circumstance and ended up losing your shirt, all the while thinking so highly of yourself as we tend to do, then maybe you aren't as brilliant or special as you initially believed. And unlike the real competitor, who takes losses on the field in stride because he lives in terms of seasons within an overall career, we stand appalled and offended by this shocking verdict.

Why? Because we're trying to win the Super Bowl all the time without ever getting our own uniform dirty. In our grandiose delusion we've already got the victory parade planned out, and maybe earmarked some of that hypothetical prize money for a boat we'd like to purchase. But when there's no middle ground in your plan, even a small dose of realism can make you crumble to the floor like a child having an epic meltdown.

We gamblers need to accept that behind our compulsive habits and unreliable instincts, there has always been a crucial design flaw in the blueprints which doomed us to failure at the structural level. It's time to wire up this condemned casino and initiate a controlled demolition of our quixotic illusions before anyone else we care about gets hurt.

We've got to find the strength to walk away like regular people do after a business venture fails. We would also be wise to learn how to forget, just as the best football cornerbacks train themselves to have no memory of the last play after being burned for a big gain by the opposing team's wide receiver.

Let go of the past. Set your baggage down. A better tomorrow is waiting for us all, I promise you.

21. LOVE AND OBSESSION

When I compare the life I have to the life that could have been, one of my greatest regrets is that I let the woman who truly loved me walk out the door. I was simply unable to choose her over gambling – and never could I have imagined how progressively bleak and lonely my existence might become as the years passed.

Which is why every gambler will tell you that of all the things you lose due to addiction, money is the least of it. This mindset that's fixated on being in action causes you to prune away the many possibilities life has to offer, from the lightest of sprigs to the heartiest of branches, until all that's left is the trunk standing naked and bare.

Then it's just you and the blackjack dealer facing each other down on the casino floor, flipping cards and trading chips back and forth for hours. That's the cool version, by the way, like a scene from some 1990s Tarantino movie. More often, the life consists of you poking around your phone to place a bet or check on the ones that are incubating…

I met Karla for the first time at one of my parties at the Parkloft Condos where I lived in San Diego. It was the ultimate bachelor pad because you could actually see the Padres games being played inside Petco Park from my balcony. People were always stopping by in the evenings for drinks and to enjoy the view.

She and I immediately hit it off and for seven years she put up with my shenanigans for the greater good of our relationship. Was she stupid? No, she was in love. With me. While I was obsessed with gambling.

The selfless versus the selfish.

The heart versus the ego.

Fantasy versus reality.

Me versus us.

I was making a million dollars a year and had a woman who wanted to take care of me, but my mind was elsewhere. I neglected her, our relationship, even basic responsibilities like paying rent. We got evicted from our apartment and went to live with her parents who had a tiny place over in the Little Italy neighborhood.

Despite everything, Karla always had my back. She went to Gamblers Anonymous meetings with me, and didn't even flinch when the bookies and loan sharks came sniffing around. But still I took her for granted. Nothing she did was ever enough.

Why? Gambling was just stronger. It was my true love. Sometimes she would say, "You're cheating on me with gambling." All I could do was shrug, because she was right.

She told me so many times, "If I catch you gambling again, it's over." My response? Get sneaky!

In the morning I'd walk into the kitchen and open the fridge, then pretend to poke around the shelves while holding my phone inside and placing bets. But she was no fool. When she came in and asked what I was doing, I'd tell her I was looking for the mustard. She'd shake her head and say, "Nope, you're busted!"

Karla's the only woman I've been with who deeply cared about me – and that includes the one I was actually married to for eight months back in 2002. She must have given me half a dozen chances. If I could do it all over again I definitely would have tried a lot harder to change my ways.

When Karla finally left, she was just done. I'd neglected her to the point that she was able to put up a stone wall and walk away without shedding a single tear. There was no doubt in her mind about the decision to go.

But she didn't win, she escaped. We both lost because of me. She moved on because she had to. I didn't, because I couldn't.

Being a degenerate gambler means constantly roping people into your dramas, schemes, and the latest urgent crisis. Whether it's family, friends, or business associates… eventually we drag them all down. When you want the whole world, you never appreciate the little things in life. He who would be king can't even keep a houseplant alive.

Karla's out there somewhere living a real life with her family now. Raising the kids, driving them to school, maybe taking them to dance class or baseball practice. I'm still doing what I always do, making picks on all the same teams that I've thrown millions of dollars at in a losing effort. Building nothing, learning nothing as time plods along.

In the end, Karla realized she had to cut her losses. She had to give up on me because I was unwilling to make an honest effort at giving up the gambling. I lied to her. I brushed off her concerns. I humiliated her and put her through hell. And on that day when she said goodbye for the last time, within minutes my face was buried in my phone looking for more bets.

In the battle between love and obsession, obsession always wins. But the victory is hollow because you never have anything to show for it. Love, meanwhile, gets beaten to a pulp and limps away to a safe place while it heals. The human heart that dares to love unconditionally can mend itself after being broken, whereas the heart that remains impervious to both fire and ice simply fades into nothingness through disuse.

I hope it's not too late to have something that resembles a normal life one day. I want to get back into shape and host backyard barbecues again. I'd like to coach youth sports instead of bet on games.

I yearn to experience life's joys, to laugh and share good times with someone special like a teenage romance.

Who knows, maybe Cupid in his infinite and playful wisdom will be more generous with me than his cruel cousin Lady Luck...

22. PREDATORY PROMISES

Are you familiar with those guys who advertise their "lock" picks? They're the ones in the slick TV spots and paid radio segments claiming to be so confident in their abilities that they'll give you a winner for free.

Confident indeed! Because they're confidence men who have built up million-dollar empires by roping in gullible people hoping to make a quick buck betting on the games.

Plus with smartphones and the internet, these charlatans can reach even more people directly on the cheap. Throw on a suit, hire a couple of hot young models, film the pitch, then find a kid who's good with graphics on Fiverr or Craigslist to edit the thing. Boom, now you've got a slick promo you can post around social media for free.

Behold the declarations of gambling glory made from the predictor's pulpit, as they whip the audience into a craven frenzy with the words, "I have seen the way. Follow me and God will rain money down upon you."

Just be sure to send a little cash their way first to help grease the skids...

These so-called experts have driven people to bankruptcy, divorce, prison, and suicide. They are frauds!

What's funny is I knew a couple of these predatory preachers of the false promise back when I lived in Vegas. Sometimes I'd even see them at Gamblers Anonymous meetings because they'd gone broke – again. That's right, the guy who says he's gonna lead you to the Shangri-La of sports betting nearly ended up on the street because of his own crappy track record making picks.

I will say this, however. What they did have was a plan, a *business* plan. Didn't make any sense to me at the time and I told them as much, but today they're roping in dupes by the thousand while I'm still out there chasing glory one bet at a time.

I guess they figured out just enough about human psychology and then created a niche for themselves within the ecosystem they were most comfortable with. Sports! The action! All the thrills and spills!

They approach a mark and present themselves as someone not much different from you, who just so happens to have a few extra passes to the VIP lounge.

"Hey, buddy. How does all-access sound? Come on in, friend..."

What a crock! But it works, because everybody has little vulnerabilities that can explode into chasms of pain if manipulated by skilled operators. Who doesn't like easy money? Who isn't looking for a shortcut now and again? Who doesn't want to be showered with praise while presenting an image of success?

All you gotta do is just put a little on the line. What's five bucks? What's fifty for a chance at two hundred?

You feel pretty darn smart when you pick right, so you might as well have another go. Meanwhile if you lose that first bet, you'd prefer not to call your own judgment into question. *Some* sort of fluke must be the reason you lost, so you place a second wager in that instance as well.

That's why casinos still offer the nickel slots and make a big show of it anytime someone hits the jackpot. The point is that they've got you gambling. You're in *their* arena doing their thing. You're directing your attention and energy toward their vision of the world. They'd be crazy not to throw you the occasional bone and say what a good boy you are!

Which makes the way I gamble even crazier – that much sicker and sadder. I slink in and out of a tacky restaurant that serves as my "casino" a couple dozen times a week, and there's no free drinks or cute girls wishing me luck along the way. When I lose, I don't have any exciting memories to show for all the grief I've incurred, cither.

And if I happen to win, rather than a barrage of flashing lights and jingling bells, the restaurant owner testily counts out the hundreds and stuffs them inside the type of paper bag that the winos use to conceal their 24-ounce cans of beer. Nope, not too glamorous.

In essence, I suppose it's really not much different from the folks you see sitting alone tapping away at a bright screen amid a sea of flickering gaming machines. The lifers. The addicts. The rats who got hooked on pressing a lever to receive food decades ago. Spiritual forebears of us zombies gambling day and night on our smartphones. Forever trying to outsmart a computer algorithm that was designed to keep them playing while also keeping the casino lights on.

Tap, tap, play. Tap, tap, pay. Crush out cigarette and repeat.

At least what I do involves a true element of chance: the human factor. You never know when the high-pressure play on third down might turn into a sack-fumble rather than just a sack. Anything can happen when a round bat swings at a round ball that's traveling nearly a hundred miles per hour. The blade of a hockey stick, when held against the ice at a slight angle by a kid who learned to walk on some frozen Canadian pond, can deflect a slap shot from the point and thus reroute its trajectory by a few degrees, so that the puck beats the stoic Finnish goaltender's outstretched glove. That's what I'm talking about!

Of all the projects, activities, and investments in life, I find that nothing's more exhilarating than the pivotal moments which determine the outcome of a game. Nothing compares to the intimate visceral thrill you feel as everyone's fate – from the players to the gamblers to the fans – hinges on that dimpled leather ball jangling around the basketball rim. It's breathless drama as worlds turn on the axis of the smallest details... What else can top that?

Sex? Maybe! But when the act of love can be bought by the hour and hearts turn cold after the slightest misstep, sometimes it makes more sense to abandon courtship for the courtside seats, where at least the rules are set and you know how long the competition will last.

Like most guys, I've dealt with too many date night rainouts where the girl who flaked just never got around to honoring the raincheck. Fool me once, shame on you. For me twice...

Well, let's put it this way. If I'm gonna play the fool in life, I'd rather chase my own tail than that of any woman whose name isn't Lady Luck.

23. MANIPULATION

The con man treats all aspects of life like a party or a big joke. He's constantly pulling sophomoric pranks at the most inappropriate times for his own amusement. He causes unnecessary drama with a grin on his face, as if to announce to the world that despite his age or net worth, he really should be sitting at the kids' table.

Who knows, maybe that's what people like us are secretly hoping for. Strip away the danger and mystique of our messy lifestyles and what's left? A self-absorbed man-child who demands to be indulged and accommodated at all times. A human tornado that refuses to stop or even slow down, let alone be bothered with learning how to cook or iron a shirt... not when something exciting is happening *out there!*

We might be close to functionally useless, forever relying on an army of service industry workers to get by as we dash headlong toward the next crisis. Each catastrophe being entirely preventable, of course, if we lived a more balanced life that adhered to the rhythms and cadences best expressed by the concept of *limits*.

Nevertheless off we go, galloping into the distance like an untrained pony, because you can't teach us anything we don't think is worthwhile... right up to the moment when it might be of use. Mature habits like politeness, respect, and accountability are usually taught by parents or later pounded into a person by life itself, but when you're stubborn and always keep a parachute handy, it's possible to avoid that reckoning with reality.

Our general attitude toward daily life is fraught with an undercurrent of antisocial fatalism. In the depths of our being we feel terribly alone and have no faith that with a little trust and cooperation, we might all lead better lives.

Our manipulations are subtle, but really not all that sophisticated. We steer conversations like a parent using a plush toy to placate a crying child after bumping its head. We beguile our prey in the same manner that a horny guy maneuvers his date into the bedroom as quickly as possible.

Distract and screw, that's us.

Always angling to get what we want, other people's feelings be damned. What they represent in that moment is nothing more than an obstruction we're trying to turn into an opportunity which can be seized upon. And don't you dare protest or call us out, because this is a one-way street, pal. We're gods and you aren't even human. Gimme, gimme, gimme is the law of this land!

When we call, we expect you to pick up after the first ring and then come running to our side. When you call us, we'll get back to you if and when we feel like it. Our excuses are valid, your concerns trivial. In our minds, it's the user versus the loser... when in fact *we* are one in the same.

There are loopholes in our character that enable us to feel no compunction about abusing legal technicalities or people's innate goodness. But the person who's victimized, even if they allow it, can always start saying no at some point. They aren't the ones whose souls are corrupted. It's not them plotting to wedge their way into someone's life in order to pilfer the goods.

At worst they're meek or naive, and those who are aware of what we're up to might actually be savvier than we give them credit for. They pivot and cede ground as part of a martial arts dance to avoid getting hit with the fatal blow – all the while knowing that our own momentum will eventually swing around to bring disaster upon us instead.

So enjoy those petty victories while you can, fellow scammers and liars. The pride we feel for sniping illicit gains is nothing more than when schoolboys giggle after getting away with stealing candy from the drugstore. The point is now we're hooked on sugar, and they're counting on us to pay them back for that one freebie over the course of a lifetime.

As for all the rubes wandering around in gullible bliss, so what if they remain susceptible to being taken in by our wiles now and again? More often than not, they encounter other honest souls along their journey. Together they live peaceful lives full of so much prosperity – in every sense of the word – that they barely even notice the bruise after bumping into the likes of us.

Which is why their cup runneth over while we always seem to look down into empty hands, no matter the size of our latest score. Where we've gotten life all wrong is that it's not about *what* we're doing, but *how* we go about it. We're stuck in a scarcity mindset, frantically burrowing holes into the ground like some crazed dog, earning no style points and taking no pleasure in the process along the way.

The clock is ticking on how much longer we'll be able to keep up this unbecoming charade before we're forced out of necessity to move on to the next town. Then another reset back to zero with nothing learned, nothing gained – and nothing planted.

Nope, just the endless cycle of the spiritual vagabond looking to grab table scraps from the unsuspecting, instead of behaving with enough dignity to earn yourself a place at the table. But of course, then you would be expected to handle the silverware properly and look people in the eye when addressing them.

It's a hard instinct to resist, this shortsighted sneakiness which always puts the self over principle. But until we make the decision to change, we'll forever be a jester with no court, and branded like the ignominious gunslinger that kills a rival who's asleep in bed rather than at high noon out in the public square.

We keep strutting our stuff without an ounce of shame, but remain oblivious to the whisper campaigns that close doors we never knew existed. Still we push onward, snatching tiny bites and stray nickels from the unaware, drifting further and further from our potential as we fail every test that life lays out in hopes of nudging us onto the righteous path by making the correct choice.

Do you know why the lazy man is often the most tired person in the whole world? He's exhausted after trying to siphon away the essence of those who are most fulfilled in life. Whereas all he would need to do to reach their level of contentment is just ask to stand by their side. They would welcome him gladly, confident in the knowledge that the world is a better place when you're not always glancing over your shoulder.

Will we ever have the courage to stop scuttling around in obscurity and approach our fellow man with hat in hand?

24. TELLING TALES

Today on a work call I told one potential client that I was a single parent, when in truth I don't have any kids at all. Why'd I do it? Because the woman on the other end of the line said she was a single mother of three. I used that little ruse to help build a sense of commonality with her in order to close the sale.

I've told customers I'm an avid fisherman even though I've never held a fishing rod in my life. One guy thinks I have a singing parrot at home, and I convinced an old lady from Sicily that my grandmother was Italian even though I'm Jewish.

Anyone or anything my clients want me to be, that's who I'll be. I'm all about building rapport as soon as they open the front door – my philosophy being that if a person *has* to purchase a particular service, why not hire someone you get along with?

So I play the chameleon by telling people what they want to hear while selling them on what they need. But who else in the world can make millions of dollars peddling sprinklers besides me? No one!

The thrill that follows closing a lead isn't too far removed from gambling, in fact. A lot is riding on that fateful moment when they either say yes or no – money, pride, the health of your business. We've got mouths to feed, an Angie's List reputation to maintain, and I'm the engine behind the whole operation.

I think that if I led a normal life the rest of the time, maybe all these embellishments wouldn't be that big of a deal. But after years and years of wearing the mask, I'm starting to wonder if it's catching up to me in the same way that gambling has.

It's one thing to banter about baseball trivia with someone else who cherishes the game, but maybe I take it too far when I pretend to love their favorite team or spin a yarn about having met some Hall of Famer because I'm so eager to make the sale.

Am I really being unethical or just a bit sneaky? Either way, it can be exhausting trying to keep track of all the little fibs I've told to hundreds of people – especially when my gambling habit brings out the worst in me. Then the combined weight of all that BS and obsessive behavior merges into one giant pulsing mass of bad karma.

Bottom line, I'm concerned that I might be losing what little is left of my true self. This blurring of reality and fiction manifests in a variety of ways, both big and small. In my work I've crossed the line from salesman with a winning smile into something more cutthroat and calculating. The effort is made not for its own sake, but rather fueled by the need to get my hands on people's money so I can gamble it away frivolously.

Even if I manage to keep my life compartmentalized on the surface, I worry that negative attitudes and a sense of desperation might bleed over to poison the one good thing I've got going, my business.

I think most people with addictive personalities are terrified of losing their grip on the reins, because then the balance they've carefully crafted might spiral out of control. We've already been doing everything within our power to prop up the rickety facade we present to the world, all the while knowing that a dam will burst if it falls.

Then not only will the rot and ruin of our secret lives be revealed, but such a collapse might also provoke a total breakdown of our composure. Because despite our impulsive and degenerate tendencies, we truly have been trying to keep ourselves in check by going through the elaborate process of keeping up appearances. What happens if we *really* start letting it all hang out?

I think we know the dreadful answer to that question. Those are the times when we're at risk of taking things so far that there might not be any coming back.

A weekend-long drug binge leading to overdose. Racking up impossible debts in a gambler's last hurrah, the consequences be damned. Committing crimes brazenly with the subconscious goal of being *stopped*. Maybe even following through on that lingering urge to end it all through an act of self-destruction…

How can we be genuine when so much of our existence is steeped in sickness? Sometimes we lie not to scam anyone, but as part of an effort to pass for normal. Inevitably something manages to flush our weakness out into the light and we proceed to sabotage any goodwill that the well-meaning veneer had gotten us.

It's a paradox and a trap. We're walking on eggshells in front of the mirror, desperate to prevent the next cascade after our will falters and we make another mess of things. We swear that if we just knew what to do to get better we'd do it, but the sad fact is that a more appropriate message might be found in the 2005 movie *Lord of War*.

Nicolas Cage is an international arms dealer whose unscrupulous ways make him wealthy enough to win the woman of his dreams, a supermodel played by Bridget Moynahan. At one point Jared Leto, the younger brother Cage brings into the business, says to him, "Maybe doing nothing's better than doing this."

How can we apply such a concept without becoming nothing at all? How will we feel alive if missing out on the action is done for our own benefit? How do we convince ourselves that personal reinvention is a good thing, when it's only the *consequences* of our behavior we dislike and not the lifestyle itself?

It may be that we have no choice but to leave our fate up to the ultimate roll of the dice, because too many of us still actively court disaster despite all the fine words we recite at meetings and during therapy sessions. We truly are alone with ourselves in those crucial moments when temptation threatens to switch our brains over to self-destruct mode.

I sometimes wonder if even God is powerless to stop this runaway train of a mindset, or if the concept of free will is inadequate to fend off the demons we face.

All I can say is that I'm still standing. Alive and well *enough* to speak to you about our shared pain.

We've got to believe that if we make the effort to fight our way back above the surface, surely others will be there as well.

Together we'll form a human lifeboat and sail off in search of a new shore.

25. REBEL WITHOUT A CAUSE

For years people have made suggestions about how to put a tourniquet on the gambling wound that's draining me of my lifeblood. I'll nod in agreement, maybe even take a few steps in the right direction, but soon enough I feel the itch to get back into the action and that's that.

Part of it stems from the fact that I'm a born rebel. I've always gone against the grain, howling in protest against the constricting world of hall monitors and meter maids. My working career has proven that you don't need to cover your walls with framed diplomas and certificates to run a successful business out in the real world, either.

But if money can't buy you happiness, maybe it also can't save you from yourself or what you never learned about life. The rebellious spirit needs to have purpose and calibration, otherwise you end up confusing the friends who are genuinely looking out for you with the sadistic prison wardens.

My judgment is flawed because I've managed to use money and a stubborn attitude to insulate myself from the kinds of bloody noses that give a normal person pause. This strain of willfulness sets us up for a major downfall when excuse making or sticking your head in the sand stops working.

Then you have those days where everything catches up to you. All the facets of your life which you've neglected – like maintaining your car or your teeth or your relationships – they come grinding to a halt in rapid succession. You break down on the highway an hour after your girlfriend breaks up with you... and then the *real* you comes out in full force.

You've sworn allegiance to your addiction and nothing's going to stop you, let alone convince you to turn back around. You double down on that which fuels and defines you, clinging to it desperately like a terrified child with a teddy bear.

"The big, bad world is a scary place, but at least I have you."

You savor those comforting minutes and hours before reality comes roaring back to hit harder than ever. You feel so alive while the bets remain in limbo that you're oblivious and unprepared for when the waves crash down with loss after pulverizing loss.

I've gone through so many smashed cell phones and laptop computers it's almost a crime against technology itself, not to mention all the underprivileged children who would give an arm and a leg for one such device.

"Sorry, kid. Them's the breaks. But hey, keep kicking that old soccer ball around the dirt lot, maybe you'll get discovered one day and I'll buy your jersey."

Am I really that heartless on top of being so wasteful? I guess that's what happens when you're wrapped up in yourself, and it reveals how the losses extend well beyond dollars, people, and teeth. You end up paying for your weakness with your humanity to the point that very few allies are willing to stick around for the long haul. Oftentimes it's when we reach that place of complete and utter isolation that we finally decide to give up the ghost.

Deep inside, we've always known that it's *people* who matter the most, not the artificial euphoria promised by fame or riches or drugs. But to actually *act* on this truth, it's just so difficult to put into practice.

What's even more frustrating is that right now there are people in our lives virtually begging to lend us a helping hand, but still we won't take it! We would rather complain about our problems than pursue a possible solution in a serious manner. Our defiant nature says we'll figure it out for ourselves, and too often we end up *experiencing* every lesson the hard way, if not actually learning from it.

"One step forward, ten steps back. This rerun sure is getting stale. But no, I won't pass the remote."

Thus the daring rebel is revealed to be just another control freak who's not all that different from the kind of domineering personalities he's based his whole identity on repudiating. To give up that narrative might be even harder than quitting our habit, because at least it gives us a role to play.

The down-and-out gambler scrambling to find enough cash to enter the next big poker tournament... how exciting!

The emaciated junkie shivering and madly scratching at himself inside a detox facility... his fate hangs in the balance!

But to stand completely naked and stripped of our costume? Soul-crushing questions are sure to follow.

Who are you? What have you done with your life? Is it too late to look in the mirror without blinking, cast judgment without buckling at the knees, and then write an honorable next chapter for yourself?

I say that if we were willing to get high on our own supply of nonsense all this time, surely we can test drive a new idea without getting worse results than what we've known. The ride might not be as thrilling, demanding a lot more patience while also being stingy with the rewards... but it just might deliver the kind of lasting happiness that's eluded us throughout these long years of mad chasing.

The fact is that the rebel without a cause needs to drop his act and get real, because like all men, one day the bell will toll for thee.

We should be grateful that there's still any time left on the clock for us to decide whether we pass into the next world *at* peace, or just in need of it.

26. HIDING IN THE SHADOWS

We have so much potential but we've got our priorities all mixed up. We're like rogue soldiers who've gone out to raid farmhouses instead of quietly meditating on the eve of an important campaign to capture a city. We indulge petty selfish instincts for years until our schemes and crimes embody the mantra "go big or go home."

Or go to jail, as happened to a guy I know who embezzled millions of dollars from one of the most successful female singers of our generation. Because he just couldn't help himself. Couldn't reach into the cookie jar for a taste and stop there. He got used to living large at his client's expense, and only recently wrapped up a stint behind bars where the rooms were anything but large and the commissary cookies tasted oh-so bitter.

What's that I keep saying about the tortoise and the hare?

It's all well and good to discuss this stuff after the fact or when it involves someone else. But when you're the one actually caught up in it, working a job and paying taxes and having a social or family life... The pressures and obligations can quickly pile up. You feel trapped and think you have to keep going, because the embarrassment you'll experience after voluntarily pulling the emergency brake seems worse than what might happen when you're found out.

What are the root causes of this *urge* that drives us headlong toward negative outcomes? I don't think it's as simple as saying, "Gamblers subconsciously want to lose." The hell with that, I love winning! But you *could* say that I savor the danger even more. Being in the fray with everything on the line. Yeah, that's living right there.

We need to dig deeper to see what's really going on inside of us. Why are we not content with all the luxuries of modern life that can be had simply by working a normal job? Is it greed fueled by envy? Or is that also too generic a diagnosis?

Maybe it's not enough to lay the blame on pride or hubris, either. No, something much bigger and more sweeping is going on here. Our lack of discipline aligns with the flaw in our overall vision, which then creates a fragmented worldview where we feel detached from a meaningful identity that might persuade us to stay grounded.

I feel like I'm probing blindly to find the words that describe our peculiar brand of alienation. For example, I don't really practice the religion of my birth. I'm also not a big patriot who participates in local politics or even goes to Fourth of July parades. There's no grand historical narrative inspiring me to walk the straight and narrow path, no great building project to assist as a member of my community.

Granted, these things still do exist in the world, but

they're just on too small of a scale for hyperactive people like me! The idea of joining the local congregation makes me sick to my stomach because it all seems so banal. Why is that? Because I'm better than they are! I was born for more than listening to boring sermons while sitting next to people I don't really like or ladling out soup for the homeless on Friday nights.

When you grow up watching MTV and Hollywood blockbusters, then later move to Los Angeles and find yourself surrounded by all that energy, how could you expect to live humbly and *not* veer out of your lane like my pal who stole a celebrity's fortune?

They say no man is an island, but the way we addictive personalities live seems to flaunt in the face of that maxim. We've established cults to ourselves on these isolated atolls as compensation for our feelings of inferiority and to shirk blame for our behavior. We shake our fists and shout, "Who dares to question the ways of God?!"

Only after we're swamped by the hurricane which fed on the detritus of our foul deeds do we limp back to the mainland in search of sanctuary. We lament that we failed without actually regretting what we did, all the while begging those we resent to help us.

The churches and temples. The therapists and mental health counselors. The discussion groups filled with fellow washouts who are redirecting their energy toward weaving a net strong enough to catch our fall.

We begrudge them because we still haven't accepted defeat. No, the plan is to use them just long enough to get back on our feet, then go racing back to the island where we are all-knowing and set the rules. There we will bask in our self-professed glory without judgment or having to contribute to anything that's outside of us or greater than ourselves.

With every small advantage obtained in this surreptitious manner, we end up stealing that much more from who we could be. The subsequent loss of trust and goodwill is never worth the meager immediate gains because it takes so long to earn back, if ever. Even then we subconsciously take into account that there's always a new mark around the next corner, always another town we can move to if the situation gets too dicey.

If that's not the kind of hollow, shortsighted victory which typifies a childish mindset, I don't know what is. We truly do want to be unassailable like some comic book deity. Money, drugs, fame… *something* exists out there which, once possessed, we believe can lift us above both fallibility and obligation.

To be loved unconditionally, without context, and not for who we are or what we've done.

The problem is, only the true God of the universe can offer that. Solely relying on people or chemical substances or the myth of oneself will inevitably let you down. Who's going to stand by your side when the money runs out, the drugs wear off, or your body fails?

On this grand stage where the human comedy unfolds, eventually we all experience that one moment of overwhelming clarity when the deepest truths are revealed to us. But for far too many, this comes too late to act upon by changing the course of one's life. While we may at last finally feel a sense of grace, we also die with heavy hearts regretful of the wasted opportunities and potential left unfulfilled.

Variations on this preventable tragedy play out in every city and town from coast to coast, often in shameful and isolated silence. I've decided to speak up in the belief that we cannot allow ourselves to be left for dead simply because our pride got in the way. There's so much we could build and give, if only we could give up the lies we've been telling ourselves and the world.

A richness far better than riches awaits us. A new path beckons, one that's meaningful in itself rather than merely serving as an opportunistic steppingstone *up*.

If people can't actually change their core makeup, that doesn't mean they have to stop living altogether. We just need to reroute all the manic energy that's coursing through us toward something more positive which has the potential to grow.

You can still leave a legacy that's more substantial than a cautionary tale. You can redefine what victory looks like and experience life's highs in new ways. The worst of your past can inspire a better future for yourself and countless others. Besides, we already know where the road we've been on leads, and I really don't want to wind up there.

So here's to trying something different, every day and in every way. What have you got to lose?

27. WORK IN PROGRESS

Everyone loves a success story. But how do you define that expression within the framework of a recovering addict, where the gains are often measured in bandages applied and wrong turns not taken? There's probably also got to be different criteria for each vice and then a sliding scale of evaluation depending on how far into the depths you've sunk.

I think that susceptibility to temptation and recidivism remains high due to our inherent nature, and so speaking in absolutes might at times be discouraging enough for some of us to fall off the wagon completely. Which is why I like the phrase "work in progress" a lot better. It's more realistic while also being hopeful.

Maybe the fact that I'm not a licensed mental health professional means I can get away with advocating for the gray area, but let's also be honest about our situation. We aren't saints. We know what we like to do. And we sure as hell know how to tell other people exactly what they want to hear.

So again, saying I'm a work in progress seems more accurate and honest than setting myself up for a deluge of repercussions if I prematurely utter the words, "I'm cured."

That's some unvarnished truth right there! This simply isn't the time to sugarcoat anything with pleasant-sounding platitudes because our lives have been absolutely dismantled by addiction. But if I seem harsh, I'm also being fair. Critically assessing the results of our life choices is not the same as passing final judgment and then throwing away the key. We're capable of so much self-improvement, but it won't happen overnight or with the flip of a switch.

Every vice has its own pitfalls. A gambler might not be at risk of suddenly dying like the hard-drug user, but every year plenty of high rollers jump to their deaths after getting buried under a mountain of debt. Maybe they both ought to quit cold turkey, or perhaps the gambler can get away with buying a lotto ticket once a week, I don't know.

I have wondered why it is that jumping seems to be so common among gamblers who decide to off themselves. It's got to be a terrifying few seconds while plummeting toward the water or pavement below. God knows that's what I was thinking the one time I actually wandered out onto a bridge with no intention of coming back.

It must be that your mind is so baffled in the haze of defeat that you can't even organize your thoughts to calculate a fatal dosage of pills or acquire a firearm. All you can do is seek out a method that ensures your death, which a fall from great heights will most certainly do.

Ironically, up until that last bet of your last dollar, you still believed you were going to win. Next you'd go on a hot streak and win it all back. Because *this* couldn't happen to *you!* Which is probably another reason why you didn't keep a loaded gun on standby – even if the thought of suicide always remains an option in your subconscious.

We addicts have got to live with ourselves and we've got to live with *it* – and also acknowledge that none of us are Boy Scouts. It's great to think like an idealist, but maybe the ideal road to recovery has more flexibility and rounded corners.

Forget flying, sometimes all we're trying to do is not drown.

Bend but don't break.

Live to fight another day.

Maybe picking up this book will give you some much needed support whenever you're feeling weak, lost, or alone. It can be a handy supplement to your network of sponsors and allies during the times they're not available. God knows there's no such thing as having too many weapons or teammates when you're fighting the kind of demons we've been saddled with…

Here's a thought. Picture your favorite piece of art. How many times did that painter or sculptor have to tell a visitor to their studio, "It's still a work in progress"? Probably a lot! But that's what it takes to create a masterpiece. Focus, commitment, faith, and vision.

Artists live to bring something new into the world, just as we now yearn to craft a new version of ourselves. So if you falter and slide back a bit, maybe reframe it as being similar to when the artist crumples up a sketch and tosses it away. Guaranteed, he *will* complete that painting down the road.

I know my words might sound like heresy to the

therapist who's got a wall full of fancy credentials, but our lives are so fraught with extreme behavior and destructive outcomes that I have to ask, how many times can we be expected to strip ourselves down to the beams and remain psychologically intact? For some of us, the fact that the story continues at all might be success enough.

Funny how when it's just us talking to ourselves, we can actually make astute and pragmatic assessments even while thinking in dire terms. Compare that to how we just assume every wager will go our way or the contents of the baggie of drugs we just bought are clean.

I suppose our attitudes and ways of viewing the world are also evolving as we grow on this journey of personal rebirth. Sacrifice the ego to save the life – sometimes the choice is both as stark and simple as that. Make it through the dark night and you never know what might come your way, or what goodness you now find yourself capable of creating.

So place a bet on yourself and give those dice a roll, because the game of life isn't rigged the way the casinos are. I'll take those odds any day of the week.

28. ALIEN LIFE FORM

Once again I have to make it clear that the gambling life involves a lot more than winning and losing. You bring all kinds of unscrupulous people into your orbit. You invite dangers that you're really not equipped to deal with as well.

To the layman, gambling might still hold a bit of mystique. It's fun to think about how your passion for sports could earn you some extra cash. But for the guys who run the betting operations, it's just another day at the office – and they were never all that hard-working to begin with.

So they're often impatient and quick to anger. They have no sympathy for you and feel no obligation to the customer like a normal business owner. They might *need* you but they don't really want you – all they want is your money and as I've explained, they're not particularly interested in making an honest buck.

In their eyes, you're just another mark as well as a necessary evil. You're the cost of doing shady business, where the lucrative payouts outweigh the risks and having to deal with unpleasant personalities.

Every poker table inside every casino is like a mini-bullfighting ring of dueling egos. Sometimes you're the matador and sometimes the bull, charging maliciously one moment and then playfully strutting your stuff. You savor the crowd's reactions because so much of what you do needs an outsider to witness your triumph and glory. But all too often, they watch us crap out after being gored upon the horns of our own reckless vanity.

Eventually, after so many losses, what the audience once thought of as courage starts to look more like the foolhardy insanity of a child who refuses to learn. But very little about this life is child's play because you really are putting your neck on the line. Even when you're not actually at risk of physical violence, squandering the money that's supposed to go toward paying monthly bills puts you in a perilous position. Once the first domino falls, it could start a cascade that crushes you while you futilely attempt to stop the bleeding.

The Leo Tolstoy parable "How Much Land Does a Man Need?" truly does remain pertinent after all these years. It reveals how any person, no matter their station in life, can be driven to madness by greed when presented with the opportunity to have *more*.

In the story, a man is offered as much property as he can stake off in a complete loop from sunrise to sunset. He abandons the route he had initially planned as successive waves of covetousness cause him to widen his path of land acquisition, but later dies of a heart attack while racing against the sun to get back to the starting point. In the end, all the land he required was the space to bury his body.

How many times has a gambler's frantic urge to scoop up mansions around the world cost him the one roof he currently calls home? This hearkens back to that hit song by the '80s hard rock band Cinderella, "Don't Know What You Got (Till It's Gone)." You don't fully appreciate the life you've built, nor how much harder you'll have to work just to get back to where you were.

Now don't get me wrong, setbacks are inevitable in life, and there's no shame in having to regroup after swinging for the fences on a venture you truly believed in. That tests your resolve and builds character, especially when you know in your heart you left it all out on the field.

. But to lose everything in the pursuit of trivial goals, squandering thousands of dollars on meaningless games being played in leagues no one has ever heard of... that is the complete opposite. You really have to start asking yourself, why?! Why am I doing this? Why do I take the money I work so hard to get and then throw it at literally nothing?

If I bought exotic whiskeys or brand-name leather jackets, at least I'd have *something*. Something to look at or use as a conversation piece. But to habitually fail as a gambler the way I do, who wants to hear that bizarre confession?

"Hi. Yes, I did lose two thousand dollars on Scandinavian women's curling over the weekend."

"Why?"

"Umm... because I had the money."

"Are you a fan of the sport?"

"Nope. Don't even understand the rules."

"How did you know which team to bet on?"

"Apparently I didn't."

"Oh."

Followed by an uncomfortable silence. Which is a form of shock because they suddenly realize they're dealing with an alien life form – something sick or threatening that doesn't present the normal warning signs like festering boils or a weapon on the hip. I look just like them, a spiritual leper hiding in plain sight, a corrupting agent standing in their midst.

They're fascinated to a point but always careful to keep their distance. We elicit disgust because something about us instinctively raises alarm bells in the average person. We are to be feared, although they don't quite know why.

I do. Our existence is an outward manifestation of the deepest, darkest pools of human corruption, of the soul led dangerously astray. What we *live* also resides somewhere within themselves – for now safely restrained inside a padlocked trunk, but without the guarantee that one day they too might not lose all control and see that awful force unleashed.

If it can happen to someone who looks as normal as we do, that's what scares the hell out of them: their own lives are much closer to chaos than they ever realized.

So when they wish us luck on the next crazy bet, just remember they're probably hoping that in victory we'll be able to stuff that damned monster back down into the depths. Then they can try to forget they ever knew it existed.

29. PANNING FOR GOLD

For all the money I've squandered gambling, I really think that *time* is my biggest loss. I used to work out, have meaningful friendships and relationships, but slowly I stopped living and am now a complete slave to this addiction.

It just takes and takes and takes, but it never gives back.

I make the soil flourish through my lawn care business while my personal life has become a barren field through neglect. I once dreamed of so much. Living a picturesque life full of yachts and mansions and smiling people. Being surrounded by human warmth and sharing good times. The vision in my mind was so sweet, an endless vista of hope... where has it all gone?

Gambling, like every vice, possibly stems from man's inability to turn the other cheek. We can't walk away from defeat, humiliation, titillation, or an insult. We can't distinguish between the importance of answering the bell when life demands courage, versus taking the bait and foolishly chasing after the Pied Piper.

If you lose your arm in some freak accident, then you have to accept this new reality for the rest of your life. But losing your shirt time and time again while betting? Bring it on! We'll never learn, never stop, never unilaterally surrender.

Meanwhile Major League pitchers have no such luxury. Their win-loss record is printed on the back of baseball cards for all time. The most successful pro football coaches will have a career winning percentage above sixty if they're lucky.

What true competitors all have in common is that they *do* something with their defeats. They gather up that oozing mass of bile and forge it into more spin on their curveball, or a new passing play for the tight end – anything *different* from what they were doing before.

Why? Because they're professionals, not addicts. They can get past their own ego, putting the moment of disappointment behind them and preparing for the next game. They accept that there's no one to blame but themselves for throwing the hanging slider that the batter swatted over the left-field fence.

What inspires them to make the mature decision instead of deflecting responsibility or refusing to adapt? It's the fact there's a dozen hungry guys honing their skills down in the minors gunning for that slot on the big-league roster.

The narrative is completely different for an addict. Excuses are our fallback. We've got a clown car loaded with reasonable explanations for our self-sabotaging behavior. Then we kick the can – it's always next week that we'll quit or pay you back. Although we *know* better, maybe we don't actually want to *get* better. We'd rather do whatever it takes to prove that we were right all along.

As a result, my own gambling laboratory has turned into a madhouse. What was once me testing various statistical hypotheses now requires the constant mobilization of sophisticated defenses to shield that first failed proposition.

I'm smarter than everybody else. I can predict the future.

And yet, I didn't foresee that at age fifty-one I'd have nothing to show for the millions of dollars I've earned but a path of wasteful destruction for myself and others around me. As I endure this endless nightmare of exasperating and crushing defeats, my very spirit begins to give way... until finally the road ahead becomes quite clear.

It ends in insanity, prison, or death. There are no exits, no emergency pull-offs, no tow trucks coming to the rescue. You must abandon the vehicle altogether because it's a death trap that no one can maneuver safely.

You've got to have the humility to walk away. You've got to accept that some people are making money in the gambling world, but it will never be you. Winning now means no longer feeding them your lifeblood, your spirit, your time, or your savings.

You were born for more than to serve as a warning to others. The point of liberating yourself is not just to huddle in a circle with your fellow addicts telling sob stories, but to move on from the traumatic life of mental slavery.

It can be very dispiriting to acknowledge that not only is no one coming to save you, but more and more traps are being laid around the country as cities and states legalize gambling to feed their own addiction: tax revenue.

No version of the Declaration of Independence is being put forth in your name, either. Bootstraps and group meetings seem to be the addict's only recourse, as well as dramatized renditions of lives spent out on the firing line.

It's powerful to hear the unvarnished truth when one sick man lays his soul bare, as singer Layne Staley did so evocatively on the 1992 Alice In Chains album *Dirt*. Sadly, he was unable to conquer his heroin addiction and died alone in an apartment some years later. He was so stuck, so adamant, so unreachable, that even the bandmates he had conquered the world with had no choice but to let him brood with his demons.

That's how formidable any compulsion and addiction can be. It's beyond logic, beyond individual will, a force so diabolical that it emboldens you while it kills you. You can't cure yourself alone because it *wants* you to be alone!

The paradox of this test deepens even further when you see that the path to healing starts by acknowledging the opposite of what you believe as a core tenet: you must admit that you are weak, powerless in fact, and have no self-control.

Doing this does not instantly bring feelings of liberation. Instead it opens the door to the ultimate existential crisis of all. If everything you based your life upon was in error and led to a string of failures, then what about you is worth salvaging at all?

This revelation might cause you to feel even more despair as the urge to disappear or relapse comes on strong. You figure, why not at least get back to the chase if you're already beyond redemption? This is a painful but vital part of the detox process, excreting the drug of your own delusions while panning for those wonderful flakes of gold that constitute your purest soul.

It's got to be worth it. You've made it this far and you know you want to be free. So do I.

Now I'm testing a new theory in my lab: that one book written from the heart can keep millions of dollars from being cashed into chips at the new casino they built just for us down the street.

EPILOGUE: LIGHTHOUSES

Saying that you want to change your life is an act of good faith. Taking the first step then plants a seed. Combined, there's no telling what kind of magic the effort will unleash.

My story is proof positive of that. All I knew is that I needed to do something different – never could I have imagined that this urge to improve myself would later turn into a book whose butterfly effect might leave a legacy of healing for others also suffering from addiction.

If that can happen for me, the know-it-all with cotton in his ears and a ready excuse on the tip of his tongue, then imagine what your own move toward the light might accomplish. While the specific outcome of your journey may not yet be a "sure thing," there's something to be said for that old sports adage, "That's why they play the game."

You're getting out of your comfort zone to place a bet on yourself, so how can you possibly lose? It might not be glamorous or get you written up in *People* magazine, but those closest to you are definitely going to notice the difference.

Once you stop the bleeding, then you're on the path to start leading!

As weak as you may sometimes feel, there's always someone else out there more desperate for a hand up. If we can all link arms and hearts and minds, then surely this monster which preys on people during their weakest and most isolated moments will no longer have so much power over us.

A dropped football in a game being played far, far away shouldn't be able to affect my happiness. The flop of a playing card shouldn't determine whether I live or jump off a hotel balcony to escape financial ruin.

Gambling promises so much glory and yet consistently delivers nothing but agony. It's a tempting mistress that draws us in with sweet whispers, then holds us captive like an abusive partner who always knows when to sprinkle a little sugar to keep us coming around. But not anymore...

Although, I must be clear in stating that it would be naive to expect we can all just quit cold turkey. Each and every one of us has made that promise in the past, maybe even done well for a while, before something invariably caused us to fall back into the soup.

What we're doing here today is building a new lighthouse to help guide our fellow travelers through the murky waters of their subconscious and avoid getting wrecked upon the rocks. We'll live to behold another dawn and seize this blessed chance at making tomorrow better and brighter than anything we've ever known.

We'll savor the gift and pay it forward, maybe even learning to go easy on ourselves along the way. Besides, no one earns their halo overnight. First we stop making a wasteful mess, then take some time to smell the roses. Afterward, when we're refreshed in body, mind, and spirit, we can start thinking about how to embark upon something that's both wholesome and new.

I believe in you now because I once chose to believe in me, even when the odds said I shouldn't and it would've been easier to just throw in the towel. So behold the new me… and get ready to meet the new and improved you!

THE END.

ABOUT THE AUTHORS

Joel Soper grew up in Livonia, Michigan, the youngest of four siblings. After graduating from Western Michigan University he moved to San Diego, California. For nearly three decades Joel has run some of the most successful residential landscaping businesses across Southern California. He currently lives in Los Angeles.

Philip Wyeth is the author of seven novels and also has extensive experience as a copywriter and editor. Originally from Northern Virginia, he has called Los Angeles home for over twenty years. He's a film aficionado and enjoys playing golf in his free time. His website is philipwyeth.com.

CPSIA information can be obtained
at www.ICGtesting.com
Printed in the USA
LVHW110732090522
717695LV00001BA/6